Synergy "WOW" Factor!

BRING THE "WOW" FACTOR!
INTO YOUR BUSINESS AND
EARN CUSTOMER LOYALTY
FOR LIFE

CHRIS ALEXANDER

Copyright © 2025 SYNERGY "WOW" FACTOR!:
Bring the "WOW" Factor! into your business and
earn customer loyalty for life
by Chris Alexander.

All rights reserved. Printed in the United States of America. No part of this publication may be reproduced, stored in a retrieval system or transmitted in any form or by any means, electronic, mechanical, photocopying, recording, or otherwise, without the written permission of the publisher.

Project Credits:
  Edited by: Linda Coss
  Graphics: Shand Coetzee and Maryna Alexander
  Publisher: 1+1=3 Publishing, Orange County, CA. USA

Books for Business and Personal Growth
SynergyTeamPower.com
First Edition
Library of Congress Cataloging in Publication Data
Alexander, Chris
Includes biographical references and index.

Praise for Synergy "WOW" Factor!

"Thank you for the incredible sessions you led at our recent ChargeUp event, our team are still talking about it. The energy and engagement you brought set the tone for the entire event. We're so grateful for the expertise and passion you poured into this. Thank you!"

-Lauren Morgan, Vice President of H.R. & Administration, Loop Global

"The "WOW" Factor! exemplifies Chris's commitment to fostering Synergy within organizations. Through his insights and charismatic approach, he inspires personal growth and cultivates authentic leadership. At its core, The "WOW" Factor! lays the groundwork for building a brand rooted in trust, respect, and service."

-Maria R. Diaz, SPHR-CA, Director of H.R., Rice Services Inc., NP Mechanical Inc., and B2C Mechanical Inc.

"The Synergy team has not only been instrumental in developing our leadership, but also conducted excellent training sessions with line staff. Many years ago Synergy introduced the "WOW" Factor! throughout our organization and we still use it today to elevate the service provided to our residents. Chris Alexander is an integral part of our leadership and culture."

- Jennifer Suckiel, Executive Director, Freedom Village

"Chris is incredibly talented and adept at harnessing the collaborative powers of a team. In the 'WOW" Factor workshops he worked with our team to create the "Customer Touch Points" system, mapping the customer team member interaction from beginning to end. The results are stunning. Before Chris in 2024 we received 91 Google Reviews with an average score of 4.54. After Chris in 2025 we have received 331 Google reviews with an average score of 4.94"

-Jeffrey Pitzer, Founder and President, Town Center Laundry

"I engaged Chris Alexander several years ago to build a customer center high-performance culture and the results have been outstanding. The energy he and his team bring to every level of our organization is contagious and our staff love the "WOW" workshops."

-Tomas Lozano, Sr. Human Resources Manager, SPHR, Davis Wire

"Do you want a stronger employee - business relationships and a more unified team approach? Look no further than the Synergy "WOW" Factor! Chris Alexander discovered the practical steps of how to implement the Synergy "WOW" Factor! and wrote this unique book to energize and help teams at every level of the organization do the same. I have been to his presentations and got myself committed to the Synergy "WOW" Factor!

- Chhanubhai (C.G.) Mistry, Regional Director, ASQ Fellow (MSQA, MBA, CQM, CQE, CQA, SSBB)

"Choosing to "WOW" customers is a Declaration of Integrity and Intent to be World-class"

Also by Chris Alexander

Business Books, CDs, and DVDs:
- Synergy Team Power
- Synergy Strategic Planning
- Synergy "WOW" Factor! CD
- Synergy "WOW" Factor! DVD
- Synergy Leadership
- Joy in the Workplace
- Joy in the Workplace, CD Album
- Joy in the Workplace, DVD
- Synergizing Your Business Handbook
- Success Is Fun, Audio Album
- Synergizing Your Business, Audio Album

Personal Development:
- Creating Extraordinary Joy
- Creating Extraordinary Joy, CD Album
- Creating Extraordinary Joy, DVD
- Synergy Life Mastery, Audio Album
- Catch the Wind with Your Wings

"Choosing to build a
high-performance team.
means you have to love the idea
of winning through people.
It requires learning how to lead,
coach, nurture, and discipline
a team of super achievers
focused on a shared destiny.
The results will astonish you!"

Contents

Praise for Synergy "WOW" Factor!..*1*

Introduction..**11**
   The "WOW" Factor! Approach Works from the Inside Out............*12*
   Many Businesses Make a Costly Strategic Mistake *15*
   Customer Service is a Strategic Imperative *17*
   Why I Wrote this Book *19*

Section 1: The Big Picture **23**

Chapter One: Master the 7 Synergy "WOW" Factor! Principles **25**
   Synergy "WOW" Factor! – It's all About the Experience *26*
   Principle #1: Practice a Spirit of Synergy *34*
   Principle #2: Make Service a Personal and Companywide Value...*35*
   Principle #3: Live and Work with Purpose *42*
   Principle #4: Employ Right Thinking *46*
   Principle #5: Be a Builder of Trust *49*
   Principle #6: Show Dignity and Respect *52*
   Principle #7: Practice Triple Win...*54*

Section 2: Leadership's Role **57**

Chapter Two: Ensure Executive Commitment and Leadership..**59**
   Know the Difference between Managing and Leading *61*
   Start the "WOW" Initiative with a Clear Picture of the Destination.*65*
   Understand that you are in the Business of Directing Energy *69*
   Make your Culture a Competitive Advantage *72*
   Understand your Organizational Structure's Effect on Exceeding Customer Expectations *73*

Chapter Three: Create Goals and a Plan to Deliver "WOW" Experiences **83**
Choose a Theme and Goal that Tie Together *85*
Create Specific Goals for each Team Member *86*
Think World-Class *90*
Create a Plan *93*
Start with a SWOT Analysis *94*
Pay Fanatical Attention to Detail *95*
Align your Systems and Processes to your Goal and Culture *99*
Reward Good Performance *99*
Align Finance with your Goal *100*
Revisit Policies and Procedures *101*
Plan to use Technology to Support and Improve Customer Service *103*
Include your Strategic Alliances and Supply Chain *107*
Enjoy a High Return on Investment *108*

Chapter Four: Implement and Measure Your Plan **111**
"Sell" your Plan to your Internal Team *111*
Hold Regularly Scheduled Synergy Team Power Meetings *112*
Focus on the Six Most Important Priorities each Day *121*
Train your Team to Deliver on your Brand's Promise *122*
Understand that Business Measurement is Essential to Success *126*
Keep an Eye on Financial Measurement *130*

Section 3: Team Members' Role **135**

Chapter Five: Manage your Customers' Expectations **137**
First, Understand what your Customer Expects *137*
Understand the High Cost of not Living up to your Promises *148*
Use Customer Touchpoints to Manage and Exceed Customer Expectations *151*
The Customer Journey of Touchpoints *152*
Take Things to the Next Level with Extraordinary Touchpoints *157*
Deliver Personal "Oh WOW!" Customer Experiences *159*
Use Synergy Touchpoints to Handle Customer Complaints *165*
Use Synergy Touchpoints to Turn Difficult Customers into Customers for Life! *168*

Chapter Six: Put Your Customers First 173
Always Act in the Customer's Interest *174*
Develop Synergy "WOW" Factor! Awareness *178*

Chapter Seven: Be a Problem Solver 213

Chapter Eight: Examine your Perceptions about Work 223

Chapter Nine: Have a Synergy "WOW" Factor! Attitude 231
Understand why having the Right Mental Attitude is
so Important *232*
Have an Attitude of Cooperation, Collaboration, and Synergy *234*
Love what you Do *235*
Be Curious and Inquisitive *237*
Be Humble and Grateful *237*
Make it Fun! *240*

Conclusion 249

Bibliography 252

About the Author 259

Synergy "WOW" Factor!

Introduction

Have you ever said, "WOW, I just love how they cared for me! That was easy. I could do business with them again in a heartbeat!" If so, you have just experienced the "WOW" Factor! Being "WOW"ed is a magical experience. It's impressive, attractive, inspiring, and memorable—and as customers, we want to repeat it over and over.

Most of the time, when this happens, it is not by luck, chance, or fate that you were blown away by remarkable service. That service was a deliberate choice and a driving purpose of a smart and enlightened business.

Smart because the business appreciates the need for a deeper commitment to service that goes beyond the bottom line and recognizes that customer experience and brand loyalty are essential for immediate and steady growth.

Enlightened because the business' leadership chose to "WOW" customers as a core value and an honorable way to do business.

Businesses that take this approach thrive on consistent revenue increases, lowered costs, and greater profitability.

Making a profit is the goal of every business and "WOW"ing each and every customer is one of the most honorable ways to achieve it. Choosing to give every customer a "WOW" experience is a declaration of integrity and transparency to employees, customers, and shareholders . . . and it's also great for getting a steady stream of low-cost-of-sales customer referrals. The ultimate competitive advantage is highly satisfied customers who are loyal to your brand.

Smart businesses differentiate themselves from the pack by choosing to serve customer interests before self-interests and by trusting the time-honored business principle that providing true value, quality, and great experiences are the keys to repeat business.

The "WOW" Factor! Approach Works from the Inside Out

The value of service is as old as Methuselah, and it works as well today as it did centuries ago. This approach works "from the inside out," meaning it starts inside your business, with your own team members, before it moves out to the people who purchase your products and services. To put the "WOW" Factor! into action, you must first serve one another and treat fellow employees (your internal customers) with efficiency, courtesy, and politeness, just as you would treat an external customer. This creates a synergistic team climate of cooperation, support, and collaboration.

Introduction

Throwing a pebble into a pond and watching the ripples flow out from the center of the impact is a great visual of how a service culture works from the inside out.

Customer service training helps considerably in this area. Still, leadership should not make the mistake that many companies have made: believing that a training program alone will suddenly enhance service loyalty and eliminate customer complaints and problems. That is like treating the symptoms of an illness but not the cause. The root cause of bad and inconsistent service can always be traced back to the organization's culture. The values of service and quality should be practiced internally and fostered as "this-is-the-way-we-behave-and-do-things."

It then becomes an authentic outer reflection of owning "service" as a leadership and company value.

If, within the inner workings of a business, a service culture is formed and people understand that treating each other with respect, dignity, and recognition are values that are appreciated by all and practiced as a priority, then from that mindset, daily behaviors ripple out to "WOW" customers. Simply put, when an organization chooses service and respect for one another as a value and makes that an important part of the culture and job descriptions, then customer service success habits and behaviors become a natural part of daily communications. In this way, customers, guests, and trade partners are automatically and authentically treated with dignity and respect, and "WOW" service is experienced. Similarly, when leaders practice integrity by example and deliver on what they say they will do, value, trust, and commitment are established, and common goals embraced.

> *"This is the psychology of shared destiny at work."*

Let's take that notion one step further: "WOW" experiences are influenced by relationships. Relationships influence perception. Perception builds trust. And trust leads to increased sales and customer brand loyalty. Trusting business relationships rests solidly on performance. Of course, product quality and product performance are also paramount, but even the perception of quality is influenced by relationships. Brand loyalty is then reinforced when problems are solved quickly and efficiently by motivated and committed staff.

Building deeper value-driven relationships with employees and customers is the smartest way to make a consistent, steady-growing profit. Long-term, valued relationships and brand loyalty cut costs, reduce absenteeism, and increase productivity performance and profits.

Introduction

Many Businesses Make a Costly Strategic Mistake

What makes a loyal customer choose to give their business to a competitor? Who loses the sale? Is it the automated, impersonal call center, the sales representative, or the accountant who calls for payment when the check has already cleared the bank? It doesn't take much these days to lose a customer. Losing customers can devastate a business and can lead to bankruptcy. It may be a slow, steady decline, or, depending on the industry's competitiveness, the business can go down really fast. In a recent Consumer Survey, the pie chart demonstrates quite clearly the reasons why customers are lost.

For many years, business leaders have made a very costly strategic mistake: They have not made "WOW"ing the customer a "major" priority. Customer service has always been a part of strategic boardroom debates—but with a huge amount of lip service paid to it. It's as if everyone knows that service should be an essential piece and driving force of a business, but it never quite makes it to the top of the list as being most important. One of the reasons is that operational priorities are often not determined by objective, rational business sense but rather by reactive self-protective fear.

Synergy "WOW" Factor!

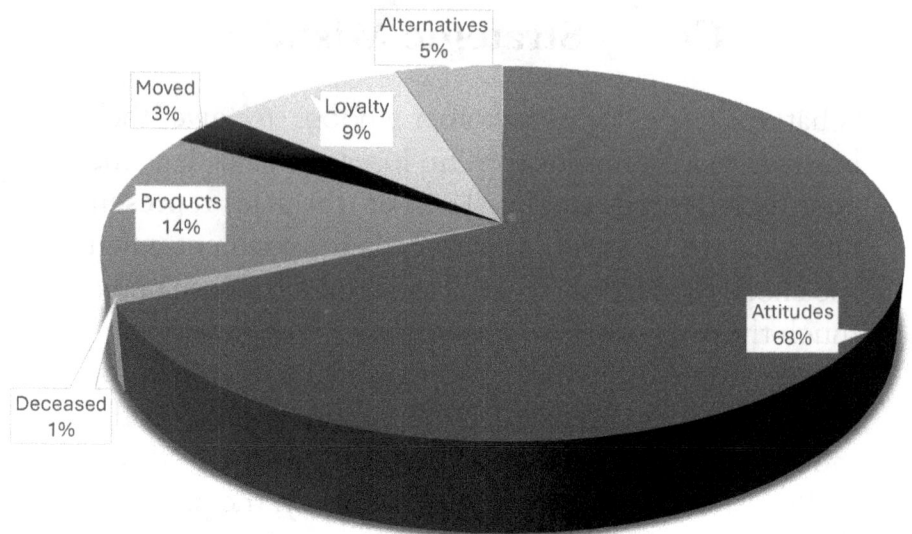

Reasons Customers are Lost
- Alternatives 5%
- Moved 3%
- Loyalty 9%
- Products 14%
- Deceased 1%
- Attitudes 68%

Let me elaborate. Suppose you see that pleasing the Chief Executive Officer (CEO), shareholders, boss, or company policies and procedures is most important to ensure your paycheck. In that case, these things will get your attention first. If your boss is deemed most important, then their needs will be taken care of as a job security priority before the customer. You and your teammates will work to "WOW" the boss while the voice of the customer becomes second and a dull noise in the background, an irritating interruption of what's considered more important work.

When the boss is the most important person in the business, relationships are based on superficial actions, jockeying, fear, and money. When service is most important, relationships expand to more than just a paycheck to a sense of purpose, higher productivity, and job enrichment.

Introduction

Customer Service is a Strategic Imperative

A second common mistake many businesses make is to see the role of customer service as a necessary/cost-bearing/defensive department strategically set up to stop the bleeding. They see it as a kind of "emergency room" to care for those inconvenient complainers, whiners, and ludicrous angry customers—anger no doubt brought on by built-in product defects or unfinished product design left to slide and financially calculated as the cost of doing business.

After years of unmet expectations, customers are weary, jaded, and on guard.

The reality is that customer service is a strategic imperative, and many organizations are finally starting to recognize this fact. Due to the economic effects of the pandemic, local and global competitors luring customers away, litigation up the yin-yang, and the grave financial adjustments needed to be made, many well-known companies have been forced to escalate service and quality to a higher executive strategic priority. They are revisiting their leadership philosophies, mission statements, systems, and processes and adding in the immense value of listening to the voice of the customer. Because of this shift in thinking, they are at last gearing up their organizational processes and culture to systematically "WOW" customers.

I hope many will permanently transform their businesses and stay in it for the long haul.

It's not only what you make but who you are, why you're in business, the way you make your products, and your purpose and values that make all the difference. Customers are fickler about whom they buy from. Service is a value; purpose-driven companies live out what they value highly. What you are deeply passionate about makes the experience more authentic. When your customers know what you stand for and can identify with your values, this creates a deeper emotional connection and enhances the perception of your product or service. "WOW" customer service needs to be one of the things that you stand for.

What customers want to know is: Do you have passion and integrity? Will you take care of my needs? Will you treat me with dignity and respect? Will you make me feel like customer service is a top priority at your company? These are things they care deeply about.

"When people care, there is magic in the air!"

"Choose service as a way of life, and life will serve you!"

Introduction

Why I Wrote this Book

I wrote this book to connect and help individuals, teams, and entire businesses who, through a service-and-servant philosophy, want to focus on delivering world-class customer experiences from the inside out, thereby building wealthy, healthy, profitable businesses and creating ongoing economic growth and job opportunities. Moreover, I sincerely believe that a service philosophy embraces all that is right with our free enterprise system. If we choose to personally embrace the notion of "first giving" as opposed to "first taking," a "how can I help you?" service mentality, I believe many of the problems of greed and dishonesty we recently experienced in our capitalistic society will be greatly diminished.

I say this with confidence because I have worked closely with executives and their teams in large and small companies. These companies trusted me to guide them through a process of organizational transformation. They allowed me the opportunity to implement several service ideas and new change-management concepts that—although I knew they would work—worked so outrageously well and so quickly that I felt I needed to repeat them in different industries for validation. In industry after industry, the results have been exceptional.

The primary concept is that business teams are no different than high-performance sports teams. Like sports teams, focused business teams "want to" bring all their individual talent and abilities to work. This approach enables them to create a safe, secure, synergistic environment, openly share ideas, and willingly focus on a shared destiny.

In this case, the shared destiny is to build an internal culture of service that enables them to "WOW" customers with ease.

A team infused with a Spirit of Synergy and focused on the psychology of shared destiny is a power source for growth and profitability.

In this book, I have paid fanatical attention to detail. Each chapter demonstrates how to engage, excite, and delight internal and external customers and build a customer-centric culture. You'll see how experiences are influenced by relationships and how relationships influence perceptions.

In turn, validated and reinforced perceptions build trust, and trust leads to communities of customers and brand loyalty. All enlightened businesses understand the importance of building trusting relationships. Trusting business relationships rely on leadership, integrity, the quality of the people, products, performance, and price, and the ability to manage and exceed expectations consistently.

Introduction

If a business promises one thing but delivers another, trust is eroded, and frustrations spread to friends, families, and business associates like a contagious disease. Through social media, unhappy customers can reach thousands of people with one single post. Any business in a competitive market relying on service to differentiate itself understands it only takes one surly employee with a "couldn't care" attitude to lose a million-dollar contract.

By choosing this book, you've affirmed that service is a core value and a reflection of your integrity. I honor that! Lets make it!=3

Synergy "WOW" Factor!

SECTION 1: THE BIG PICTURE

Synergy "WOW" Factor!

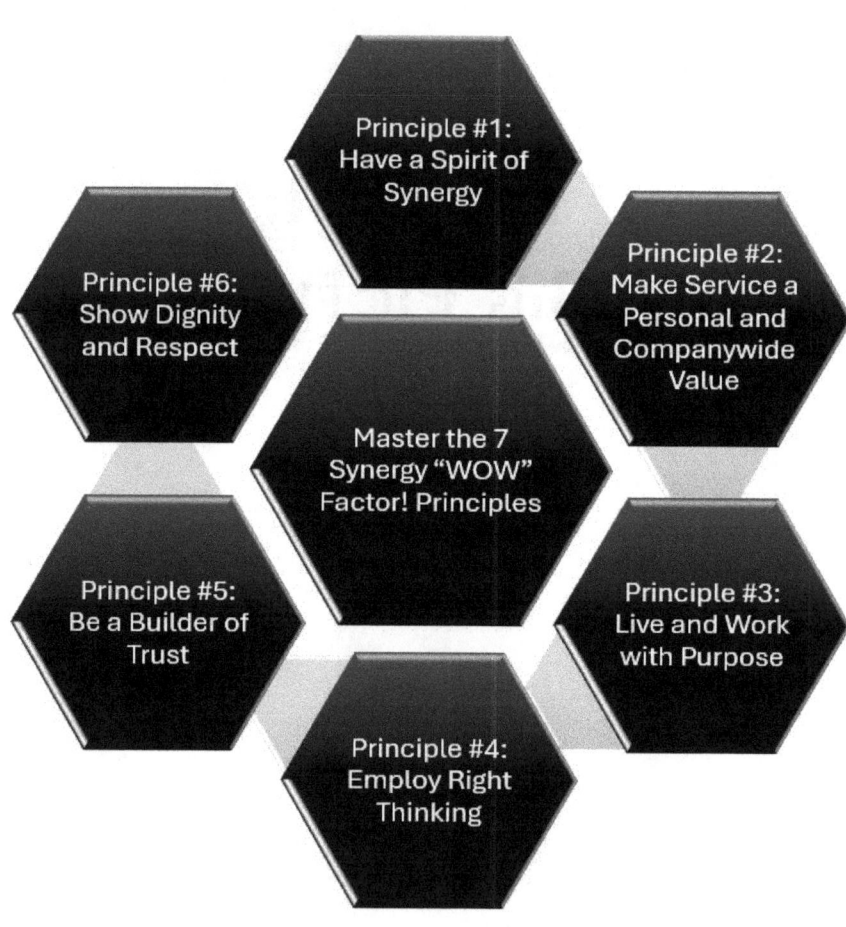

Chapter One: Master the 7 Synergy "WOW" Factor! Principles

Relationships influence perception, perception influences trust, and trust leads to the "WOW" Factor! The "WOW" Factor leads to loyal customers for life. Fusing worthy values and goals builds a mighty Spirit of Synergy that energizes individual creativity and relationships with enthusiasm, fun, excitement, and believability.

Synergy "WOW" Factor! – It's all About the Experience

"Do what you do so well that they will want to see it again and bring their friends."
—Walt Disney

The Synergy "WOW" Factor! is all about a customer service experience that surprises you and surpasses all your expectations. It makes you exclaim, "WOW!" When you experience satisfaction from a product or service, it means that your expectations have been met.

To be impressed means that your expectations have been exceeded. However, being "WOW"ed means having just experienced exceptional, extraordinary service. And when that happens, you cannot resist the urge to share your experience.

The Synergy "WOW" Factor! is experienced in many different areas of life, such as music, art, personal relationships, and, of course, in the products and services we love. For example, singers and great musicians leave us speechless and emotionally moved by their amazing talents. Sports teams can astound us with exceptional physical coordination, teamwork, and a will to win. In contrast to great musicians and sports teams, the "WOW" Factor! in business is experienced more rarely, which may be because it is much more difficult to deliver.

In a great band, when four skilled musicians are in

Chapter #1: Master the 7 Synergy "WOW" Factor! Principles

sync in a magical peak sound creation experience, it pulses out. It grabs us emotionally, connecting on a level that moves us to experience joy, exhilaration, sadness, or feel-good memories. In business, there are many variables to coordinate, including product quality, price, personalities, attitudes, and all the daily situations that can influence the customer's experience.

Creating a Synergy "WOW" Factor! experience in business is highly effective when it is done "from the inside out"—the same as a band or a great sports team. That means the value of service begins inside the company, and clear expectations are established regarding the way interpersonal communications, core values, and competency levels are coordinated, communicated, and understood by every team member at every level in every department and with every customer. Everyone is playing from the same sheet of music.

> *"No one can whistle a symphony—it takes an orchestra to play it!"*

The "WOW" Factor! is most effective when practiced by empowered people who like people and love the idea of serving others and being the best at being world-class. If you're a service-oriented person, you're one of those people who has a mindset of "first giving" behavior. You're the first to greet someone, first to say, "How can I help you," first to apologize, and first to understand that customers have a choice. For customers to be loyal, service needs to be demonstrated by initiating proactive communication as a demonstration of trustworthiness and authenticity. Those with the first giving mindset are proactive initiators who seem to "have the helping gene in their DNA." It is also important that they have the support of smart and enlightened servant leaders who trust them to make the right decisions and deliver on the company's promises to its customers. This is what Jan Carlson called "Moments of Truth".

A moment of truth results from a connection or touchpoint between a customer and a company that allows both an opportunity to form, validate, and reinforce original buying decisions and create a lasting relationship with the company brand.

There are four moments of truth. The **first moment of truth**, which takes place either offline or online, happens when a customer is first introduced to the product. It occurs within the first three to seven seconds of a consumer encountering the product, and it is during this time that marketers have the ability to turn a browser into a buyer. Procter & Gamble describes the moment of truth as when a consumer chooses a product over the other competitors' offerings.

The **second moment of truth** happens when a customer purchases a product and experiences its quality as per the brand's promise. Every time the product is consumed (used), there can be multiple second moments of truth. This provides the consumer with information for future purchases and for sharing their experience with the product/service.

The **third moment of truth** refers to the consumer's feedback or reaction toward a brand, product, or service. For example, the consumer becomes a brand advocate and gives back via word of mouth or social media publishing.

The **zero (fourth) moment of truth** is a term coined by Google. It refers to the research that a consumer conducts online about a product or service before taking any action, such as searching for mobile reviews before making a purchase. The Internet has changed how consumers interact with brands, products, and services. According to research conducted by Google, 88% of U.S. customers research online before actually buying the product.

During all of these moments of truth and touchpoints, a customer's expectations are met, exceeded, or unmet. For a customer, this is very important. This is a moment of decision validation and purchase security. This is the moment when they either fall in love with the brand or walk away. "I'm super delighted I decided to purchase my equipment from this company. My customer service advisor was great!" When the "WOW" comes together, it is a thing of beauty and awe. This is a synergy of enlightened, smart leadership, trained service teams, service as a core value, relationship power, and customer psychology all rolled into one to create customers for life.

Luka and the LEGO "WOW" Factor! Service Hero

When decisions are left to representatives with a customer-first attitude, the decisions are usually correct. The representative places the customer's needs before the needs of the manager or anyone else associated with the business. Sometimes, the decision goes against corporate dictates, but it is done solely to benefit the customer. Ultimately, the team member is generally rewarded for doing the right thing.

Chances are that when you were growing up, you had a LEGO® set. To some, it was the most cherished box in the house. To lose your favorite LEGO character was traumatic. Who else would a child turn to but a LEGO customer service agent when that tragedy happened? Which is exactly what seven-year-old Luka did.

After being told to leave his favorite LEGO at home, Luka, like most kids, took it with him anyway. Unfortunately, the toy mysteriously dropped out of Luka's pocket. Devastated, he wrote the following letter:

Chapter #1: Master the 7 Synergy "WOW" Factor! Principles

> Hello,
>
> My name is LUKA and I am 7 years old. With all the money I got for Christmas, I bought the Ninjago kit of the Ultrasonic Raider. The number is 9449. It is really good. My daddy just took me to Sainsbury's And told me to leave the Ninjago kit at home, but I took it with me and lost Jay ZX. I think it fell out of my coat pocket.
>
> I am really upset that I lost him. Daddy said to send you a letter to see if you will send me another one. If you can, I promise I won't take him to the Shop again.
>
> Thank you! :)

Despite being told not to, the Customer Service Representative (CSR) sent the boy a replacement and a surprise. Here is his response:

Synergy "WOW" Factor!

Hello Luka,

We are very sorry to hear that you lost your Jay ZX, but it sounds like your dad might have been right about leaving it at home. It sounds like you are very sad about it, too.

If you lose one of your mini-figures, we normally ask you to pay for a new one. My bosses told me I could not send you one for free because you lost it, however, I decided to call Sensei Wu to see if he could help me.

Luka, I told Sensei Wu that losing your Jay mini-figure was purely an accident and that you would never ever, ever let it happen again. He told me to tell you, *'Luka, your father seems like a very wise man. You must always protect your Ninjago mini-figures like the dragons protect the Weapons of Spinjitzu!'* Sensei Wu also told me it was okay if I sent you a new Jay ZX and that it would be okay if I included something extra for you because anyone who saves their Christmas money to buy the Ultrasonic Raider must be a really big Ninjago fan.

So, I hope you enjoy your Jay ZX with all his weapons. You will have the only Jay mini-figure that combines three different Jays into one! I will also send you a bad guy for him to fight!

Just remember what Sensei Wu said: Keep your mini-figures protected like the Weapons of Spinjitzu, and always listen to your dad.

You will receive an envelope from LEGO within the next two weeks with your new mini-figures. Please take good care of them, Luka, and remember that you promised always to leave them at home.

Happy building!
Sincerely,
Richard
LEGO Consumer Services

Chapter #1: Master the 7 Synergy "WOW" Factor! Principles

This is a real story of the Synergy "WOW" Factor! in action! Richard far exceeded Luka's expectations. He empathized with how Luka felt and, through two touchpoints, delivered two moments of truth.

Although initially advised not to replace the mini-figure, Richard was empowered by his company to make the final decision and chose to send Luka the Jay ZX (first touchpoint). Richard also knew that when Luka received his package from LEGO, he would leap for joy because of the extras included (second touchpoint). The second touchpoint excited, delighted, and surprised Luka so much that he would remember the experience for the rest of his life.

Certainly, LEGO benefited a great deal more from sending the toy than not. Richard, the "WOW" Factor! hero, understood the value of touchpoints, and used them to create a customer for life. I have no doubt that Luka will one day introduce his own children to a LEGO set. Thanks to social media exposure, this story touched the hearts of many and was reported worldwide.

In Chapter Five, you'll learn how to create a system of touchpoints. Here in Chapter One, we'll focus on the 7 Synergy "WOW" Factor! Principles, delivering "WOW" experiences from the inside out. The following principles are how you make this happen.

Principle #1: Practice a Spirit of Synergy

A Spirit of Synergy is manifested through a deep belief that by working together and joining our experience, knowledge, creativity, and abilities, we will have a much greater positive effect on our customers, company, and employees!

"1+1=3"

A Spirit of Synergy is a mindset, a heart connection, and a behavior focused on building symbiotic relationships instead of silos of conflict and despair. Synergy and service are spiritual partners; one cannot survive without the other. "WOW"ing the customer is an inside job that begins with choosing synergy and service as personal core values, a way of life, and ongoing work ethic—not a temporary option to close the deal or just something you have to do when the boss is around.

The Spirit of Synergy grows quickly in an atmosphere of integrity.

"WOW"ing your customer is a declaration of your true integrity. You are walking the talk and, through your personal behavior, showing who you are.

The goal of Synergy is to strive for the compounded, mutually beneficial gain achieved from working together toward a shared destiny. When you have a Spirit of Synergy, your goal is the customer's goal. When focused on satisfying the wants and needs of your customer, your demeanor, attentive awareness, and attitude will result in a "WOW" Factor! experience for both of you. The idea is to exceed win/win interactions through excellent communication and collaboration and to be committed to working together to create a better outcome by expanding the potential for winning to triple and quadruple wins. If your company wins, everyone wins; if your industry wins, it manifests growth, more jobs, and more demand for your product. It builds customers for life.

Principle #2: Make Service a Personal and Companywide Value

"Service is the rent we pay for being. It is the very purpose of life and not something you do in your spare time."
-Marian Wright Edelman

Do you love what you do? If you do, then your work is easier! Dealing with difficult customers will not cause you to throw your hands up in the air and quit. When you love what you do, you are more motivated, will want to learn more, and will willingly lean in instead of being indifferent or leaning away from it.

Loving what you do shows, it oozes out of every pore in your body. It's easy to serve when you love it! Choosing service as a value is easy when it comes naturally to you. When you like serving, it's a natural feeling that you want to serve others first, which is very different from one who wants to serve themselves first. Self-serving individuals may do well in service if there are enough payoffs for doing so. That's a different kind of motivation; it doesn't last as long and is not as resilient. One may say this is just human nature. So, it may seem that I am suggesting that if you don't love what you do, you should find something you really love and do it. In this way, you will serve, contribute, and give rather than self-serving and taking.

That's a nice idea and, of course, what we should all strive for. It's true for those who love to serve or have enough talent in the area they love and who can make a living that way—but it's not true for many. Many people are in jobs they don't necessarily love, including customer service. They may have inadvertently entered an industry right out of college or high school because they needed a job! In many cases, perhaps a friend suggested they work for the same company because it's a good company and it's a good job. The idea of loving it or experiencing joy from doing it did not cross their mind.

That said, research repeatedly reveals that job enrichment and fulfillment lead to greater job satisfaction and higher motivation. If you like your work, you feel less stressed, are absent less often, don't need mental health days, and don't shoot people.

You may love playing bass guitar, but are you talented enough to make a good living? You may love to paint, but is your brand of creativity loved by enough people for you to sustain yourself? Where is this leading? It leads to a vital question: If you are in customer service and don't really love it, what will you do because you need this job? The answer is to understand that you have a powerful weapon to use daily to change who you are. You can change your circumstances and ability to succeed at whatever job you are currently doing, in this case, becoming a superstar in service!

The secret? Make proactive choices vs. reactive choices. Oh, come on, it can't be that simple. Yes, it is!

> *"Life does not give itself to one who tries to keep all its advantages at once. I have often thought morality may consist solely of the courage to make a choice."*
> -Leon Blum, 1872-1950

Let's go a little deeper. Have you ever known someone who seemed to move smoothly through life, deciding early on a satisfying career, attending the right schools and internships, making enough money, meeting and marrying the love of their life, having happy children, and generally doing everything right? This person might have been blessed with early self-knowledge, a stable home, security, and a huge portion of luck. Why do some people float serenely on life's ocean while others tread water, flounder, or drown?

You've probably known people who had all the advantages and managed to screw up their lives anyway. Some people come from nothing—no love, security, or role models—yet they manage to get it together and create a happy, successful, and meaningful existence. Others come from nothing and spend their lives perpetuating their loss—blaming everyone and everything for their circumstances. What's the difference between these people? The difference is how they exercise choices.

We each have a certain amount of free will. How we choose to exercise it determines the sort of life we lead. Sure, there are things beyond our control that definitely impact us. But how we choose to respond to those things makes all the difference.

Many people are raised to believe that they have very little or no choices, that their will is irrelevant, and that the universe does what it wants, and we can like it or lump it. These folks are fatalists. They have ignored our most powerful ability, the privilege of choice. If you have faith in nothing else—no religion, higher power, or yourself—pin your faith on this one significant idea: You have the freedom to make your own choices; they count and are profoundly important to your everyday happiness and joy.

If you don't buy this, test drive it for a while. Choose today that you are going to serve your internal customers by treating them with dignity and respect. Be proactive, and choose to greet them first. Choose to serve your external customers today by being a problem-solver—lean in and see what happens. Most internal and external customers will reciprocate. Isaac Newton said, "For

Chapter #1: Master the 7 Synergy "WOW" Factor! Principles

every action, there is an equal and opposite reaction." Once you see your effect in each situation or interaction, you'll have an easier time believing that your choices matter!

How can this help you love your job? Diving deeper into exercising new choices requires letting go of the old attitudes. Therein lies the rub! Many like the old negative ways; there's always someone to blame. Misery loves company! Yes, it takes courage! The problem with not opening up by making the right choices is that you are stuck in a state of inertia. Think of Isaac Newton's first law of motion: An object at rest stays at rest, and an object in motion stays at the same speed and direction unless acted upon by an unbalanced force.

Often, a crisis, which might result from a bad decision, will be that unbalanced force that changes the motion. The loss of a job might open your awareness that new choices need to be made. It can be a hard emotional struggle or a moment of great loss. In the end, depending on how humbling the crisis has been, most choose the appropriate reaction and move forward.

Why must it be a crisis for us to learn to make better choices? Making choices is a skill that can be developed and applied in all areas of your life. I believe that when you learn how to make better choices in your life, you will also make better choices about what you value, what brings you a sense of purpose, and what will help you grow and enrich your life. Choosing values means recognizing that certain principles have stood the test of time throughout history. They are true and as valuable today as they were when first conceived. You can choose these values at any moment and perhaps learn to love what you do through them.

Choose service as a personal and work value. Albert Einstein said, "Only a life lived in the service of others is worth living." Choose to shift your mindset from self-serving to serving others.

Practice the Golden Rule. Treat others as you would want to be treated. Keep in mind that the customer is the most important person in the business. Treat them with respect and dignity. Make them feel valued and appreciated. Be responsive and listen. The most flattering thing one person can do for another is to be present and listen. Isn't that how you would want to be treated?

The Spirit of Service at the Marriott

There is a customer satisfaction story that I've heard people talk about in the hospitality industry. In my research, I found a similar version in J.W. Marriott, Jr.'s *Spirit to Serve* book that focuses on how a commitment to taking care of the customer can impact life much deeper than what our everyday lives sometimes allow us.

One day, a reservation associate received a call from an excited bride-to-be who wanted to book her honeymoon in the Caribbean. All was well, and the

Chapter #1: Master the 7 Synergy "WOW" Factor! Principles

dates were set. However, shortly afterward, she called back to cancel, and when asked "why," there was a long silence. Then, in a faint voice, she said, "My fiancé has just been diagnosed with terminal cancer and has been given only months to live." Because of his illness, they needed to marry as soon as possible and had moved their plans up. She asked if they could move their dates up to accommodate their new plans, but that week was unavailable. Moved by this woman's tragedy, the reservation associate called the general manager at the hotel in the Caribbean, and the story also moved him. He upgraded the couple into one of the hotel's luxurious suites.

Unfortunately, by now, the woman could not get flights on the airline they had chosen. At this point in the story, no one could say that the reservation associate or the manager had not gone the extra mile. However, at this point, too, values superseded job descriptions, and extraordinary service became a "WOW" Factor! The reservation associate called a different airline, and they, too, were moved by the story and immediately agreed to fly the couple to the resort for their honeymoon on a complimentary basis.

The reservation associate later received the bride's beautiful "thank you" card. In the note, she stated what a memorable and wonderful time they'd had and how this had made all the difference to her husband before he died. She said, "You will never know what you and the Marriott did for us!"

"WOW"!

Principle #3: Live and Work with Purpose

"Nothing contributes so much to tranquilize the mind as a steady purpose—a point on which the soul may fix its intellectual eye."
-Mary Shelly

Having a sense of purpose powers up every cell and thought in your body with new energy, making a positive difference in everything that you think, feel, and do.

Purpose is spiritually based because it focuses on giving, serving, and synergizing. The gift is in the giving of ourselves.

When you have a sense of purpose, you have a context for the decisions you make in your life. Purpose helps you set authentic goals and create plans that lead to self-fulfillment.

Purpose also changes your perspective and view of life by giving them depth and breadth. It lifts your sense of place in the orchestra of life. You get the connection to the meaning of life. Purpose feeds your heart and mind with the courage to confront the fear of change. Courage to let go of negative past programming (i.e., playbacks from way back) that inhibit your potential. Purpose validates your existence and builds your self-esteem in profound and exciting ways.

Because purpose is long-term, strength builds steadily

from the inside out, cooling down life's previous frustrations and rubbing off the rough edges of impatient behaviors.

No longer is there any need to be satisfied from the outside in. No longer is happiness attached to the need for new accumulations and things. Purpose moves us away from the "instant gratification" syndrome, which has been so destructive to our society.

When you achieve a sense of purpose, you receive the gifts of peace, patience, and higher self-esteem, resulting in outstanding performance levels in all of your life's activities. Happiness is no longer fleeting, temporary, or attached to an event or circumstance. It's permanently satisfying.

"Happy are those whose purpose has found them."
-Anonymous

Having a sense of purpose empowers you with a knowing that you can make a difference by simply choosing to integrate your life and move toward integrity. Having a sense of purpose builds your self-esteem, honor, and character.

Why Do You Go To Work?

So, what will give you a sense of purpose? As you ask yourself this question, you will find that purpose is achieved by satisfying the things you value highly. Values are mostly emotionally based. Purpose-laden values are very personal values that make you feel worthwhile. These very personal values individually validate you and your uniqueness. These are life-enhancing essences that create a sense of existence and worthiness.

Living and working on purpose will mean you need to get in touch with your deeper, more emotional reasons for doing things. You need to ask yourself, "What do I value highly? What really motivates me? What will get me to live a life of joy?"

In my daily workshops, I ask people every day the big WHY question: "Why do you go to work?" Nobody needs to go to work, we can get by some way.

"Money" is a common answer.

What are you going to do with all that money? "Educate my kids." "Buy a home." "Go back to college."

Purpose is always connected to what we value highly (e.g., it may be the love of our children, the value of personal growth, relationships, etc.). The trick is to identify what you value highly and work toward experiencing it. Of course, we all need money, but most of us are working to put a roof over the heads of the ones we love. If you see your work as a vehicle to bring your values to life, work will take on a higher priority. The real motivator is what the money can deliver. Money is a means to an end, but never the end within itself.

This is what will motivate you to come to work with a

sense of purpose. You won't just go to work; you will step through the door and fully engage in your responsibilities. You will take ownership of the important and relevant fact that you are the company to each customer. You represent the company, and you are the answer to that customer's problem or solution. Therefore, you are the most important person in the business.

> *"He who has a why to live for, can bear with almost any how."*
> *-Nietzsche*

Once, when I was attending a conference, I stayed at a hotel for several days. Whenever I left or returned to the hotel, I noticed a janitor happily working. He was always very methodical sweeping the floor. Because I am a student of human behavior, I couldn't resist asking him, "Don't you ever get tired of working all the time?" He flashed a huge smile at me and said, "I am an honorable man, and an honorable man keeps his self-respect intact by always doing a good job." He was really saying that you don't work for the boss. You work for the honor of maintaining and growing your own self-respect.

A number of people work on their passion part-time for years because they have to work for money during the day. They go to school at night, paint pictures all weekend, or get an internship that doesn't pay but teaches them what they need to know to succeed in what makes them happy. If, while pursuing what you love on the side, you maintain the attitude that any work is honorable if you do a good job, work can take on a meaning grander than just showing up and hoping to make it through the day. You will be living and working on purpose.

Principle #4: Employ Right Thinking

Your face and body language should be an outer reflection of an inner glow.

"Right thinking" is about knowing your customers' needs so that you can anticipate what would create a "WOW" experience for them, surprise them with this experience, and let them walk away saying, "WOW!"

The key to right thinking is to be curious and ask questions about their needs and how you can help them satisfy them. Empathizing with your customers is the most important part of getting to know them. Ask yourself, "What would it be like to walk in their shoes?" Collect as much data and information regarding their buying patterns and decision-making behavior as you can. Use this data to know them better! Analyze the information in your Customer Relationship Management (CRM) system to know where you need to improve and how you can speed up responses, order delivery, and quality. Use customer service surveys to help you listen to the voice of the customer.

Chapter #1: Master the 7 Synergy "WOW" Factor! Principles

The most important thing about surveys is continuously using the information to improve service. Don't allow anyone to justify bad service with excuses or reasons for not changing, and don't ask for a customer's opinion if you're not prepared to make improvements. When you do make improvements, let your customers know what you have done and thank them for their feedback.

> *"Know your products. Right thinking is to never stop learning."*

Increase your knowledge of your products, company, industry, and the world in general. Avoid the trap of ignorance! The more you learn, the smarter you will get within your chosen service area, and the more you will like it. "Teacher, I used to hate math but since you taught me how, I love it!" Every customer wants to deal with an expert, someone who they have confidence in, to solve their problem.

Think about it. When you call Company A, you are looking for a customer service star. The star would state the company name, her name, and the standard, "How may I help you?" in a way that would be welcoming. However, how do you feel when you get someone who is not employing the right thinking, who speaks so quickly and in such a monotone that you can't understand a word she's rattling off?

Picture this scenario. You've called a company to ask about their gift baskets. "I'd like to ask a question about the gift baskets," you say to the person who answered the phone.

What is the response? Silence. Then, a loud sigh lets you know that your lack of organization and preparation makes this person's life more difficult. Then, you get this rapid-fire speech: "Would that be the Incredible Gift Baskets, the Gift Baskets for Business, or the All-Candle and Cookie Selection?"

"Aah, could you tell me the difference between them?" you say. This time, she cuts you off! "Is this for business, friends, or you?"

By now, your blood is starting to boil, mostly because you're being treated like you're some kind of an idiot, and you're not being treated with respect or getting the information you need. You want to know what's included in each basket, the cost, and the delivery options available for your timeline. But your customer service representative has a different agenda. Maybe she's tired, someone was especially nasty to her, or they lost her paycheck, or she worked two straight shifts. But it doesn't really matter what her problem is. What matters is that she's not really listening or talking to you. You might eventually get the answers you want from her and even place an order. But there's a good chance that the next time you need to order a gift basket, you'll look at another company because you will have taken this one off your radar and vendor list.

Now let's look at Company B. The phone is answered by a cheery-sounding person who takes the time to pronounce her words and inflect them like she's talking to a real person—you! When you ask about gift baskets, she carefully explains each basket, including its contents and price, and she sounds enthused about the products. She asks how soon you want the basket delivered and explains the delivery options. She laughs at it and sounds genuine when you make a little joke. You come away from this interaction feeling happy about your purchase, clear about when to expect delivery, and positive about the company from which you just ordered. You write down the phone number of Company B and put it in your planner for the next time you need a gift basket. Company B has won your business because its CSR employed the right thinking and provided a Synergy "WOW" Factor! service.

Principle #5: Be a Builder of Trust

Be competent in your work. Be predictably responsible. Make the right choices. Be accountable. You must be trusted to do your part.

- Do you want to do business with somebody you don't trust?
- Do you want to work with someone you don't trust?
- Would you want a relationship with anyone that you didn't trust?

Of course, you don't! Well, neither does a good customer! Customers want value. They want to feel valued and are loyal to people they trust. Creating trust is a core principle for "WOW"ing your customers.

How do you create trust? Start by understanding that trust must be earned. It cannot be demanded, insisted upon, or even regulated. A trusting relationship is at the back of every "WOW" experience, and a trustworthy person is at the back of a trusting relationship.

Be a person of integrity. Always do what you say you will do. Tell the truth; don't exaggerate. Deliver on your promises. Don't over-promise; rather, give the customer a realistic true-time schedule. If you are smart about making sure you live up to what you and your company are promising, add some additional time to allow the customers' expectations to be met.

> *"Under-promise and over-deliver."*

Being trustworthy is demonstrated in one's behavior and actions. It is a state of one's character. Character and trusting relationships are essential for long-term success in the workplace.

One of the core doctrines in Buddhism is titled the Three Poisons. The three "poisons" are greed, hatred, and delusion. Besides the negative karmic effect of these three things, they also form the basis for a lack of trust and are the roots of dishonest thoughts. The greed of any sort, even greed of knowledge, diminishes your authenticity. You become unbalanced. Hatred brings about vengeful thoughts, which in turn lead to duality and dishonesty. Delusion, within itself, cannot be trusted. Many of our fears and paranoia stem from overactive imaginations.

The way to be trusted and to trust others is to follow the Golden Rule and treat others the way you want. As you will see, the Golden Rule plays many roles in providing amazing customer service! What you think affects how you feel, which plays out in your body language and nonverbal communication. If you think that others deserve to be treated well, your customers will notice this.

In the final analysis, trust is your most valuable asset. Without trust, you cannot build relationships. Remember, "WOW" experiences are influenced by relationships, and relationships influence perception. Perception builds trust. Trust leads to increased sales and customer brand loyalty—and the satisfaction in your work that will have you show up daily with purpose and joy.

"The greatest source of power a business leader has, is the committed hearts and minds of everyone."

Principle #6: Show Dignity and Respect

In retail, it's all about experience. You need to be customer responsive and have a smile on your face. You need to be present, upbeat, and professional. You cannot bring in emotional baggage and disrespectfully share it with coworkers, customers, or vendors.

The Baggage Tree

I have a very good client who owns several retail stores. What she has achieved with the "WOW" Factor in customer service in her retail stores is phenomenal! In retail, all day and every day, you are dealing with people, all kinds of people. While some are polite, others are angry or even belligerent. Needless to say, it can be very stressful. Stress can fray tempers and create snappy attitudes that can damage the company's reputation both quickly and permanently.

In creating customers for life, it's vital to build positive attitudes from the inside out and set a standard of behavior that rests on dignity and respect. Respectful, courteous, and polite behavior demonstrates that you are a dignified professional. It's all about relationships and maintaining dignity and respect for yourself and your internal and external customers. But it's hard to have a positive attitude if you bring your emotional baggage from other issues in your life to work.

Chapter #1: Master the 7 Synergy "WOW" Factor! Principles

My client remedied the problem of staff members bringing their emotional baggage to work by putting a "Baggage Tree" outside all her stores. She then called a staff meeting and laid it out. "I care for you all," she said, "but our customer is the most important person in our business. I've noticed lately that some of you are losing sight of that. You're not paying enough attention to customer requests. I found out that several of you are bringing your baggage to work and discussing it with each other instead of paying attention to our customers. To help you solve this problem, I've put a six-foot tree outside each of our stores. When you come to work, I want you to hang your baggage and negative attitudes on the tree. You can pick it all up when you leave. Trust me; it will all still be there waiting for you if you want it!"

"If you bring your troubled relationships," she continued, "your boyfriends or girlfriends, your uncles and aunts, and any other situations that will distract you, you will disappoint me, your team, and your customers. I don't want you to do that. Without the customers, we don't have a business. To 'WOW' customers, you need to be present with them. When you are present, it is complimentary and flattering. Plus, it allows you to hear points of view more clearly and solve problems more quickly, which makes the difference."

Principle #7: Practice Triple Win

Synergy triple-win is a "WOW" Factor! force multiplier. You win by working for leaders who are committed to the principle of service. These leaders have a clear vision and the emotional maturity to recognize that leading is about bringing out the individual talents of each team member. They are passionate energizers, coaching and focusing the team's combined talents toward a predetermined shared destiny. It is service from the inside out.

> *"In this way, the customer wins, the company wins and the employee wins... in that order!"*

When you are well-trained, engaged, empowered, and have job satisfaction, you are more invested in educating and giving customers exceptional service. This will reward the company with continued loyalty. Building a community of loyal customers in this way is a good reason for companies to see their training dollars as an investment rather than an expense and a drain on profits. It's a simple yet powerful way to build a high-performance, customer-driven culture from the inside out.

Chapter #1: Master the 7 Synergy "WOW" Factor! Principles

Recap of the Synergy "WOW" Factor! Principles

- Principle #1: Practice a Spirit of Synergy

- Principle #2: Make Service a Personal and Companywide Value

- Principle #3: Live and Work with Purpose

- Principle #4: Employ Right Thinking

- Principle #5: Be a Builder of Trust

- Principle #6: Show Dignity and Respect.

- Principle #7: Practice Triple Win

Synergy "WOW" Factor!

Section 2: Leadership's Role

Synergy "WOW" Factor!

Chapter Two: Ensure Executive Commitment and Leadership

Executive commitment is key to creating the "WOW" Factor! In fact, one of the most common reasons why customer service initiatives fizzle out is that service is not embraced as a value by top management. For example, executives must understand that they need training. Training is not just for everyone else. When executives don't proactively attend change management seminars and workshops, the commitment to making the customer the most important person in the business does not stick and is not carried forward to victory. When leadership makes a strategic shift in thinking and models and champions service with passion and integrity, then employees see the level of ownership and their mindsets shift. Right-thinking behavior and actions follow. (Synergy "WOW" Factor! Principle #4)

Leadership has the influence and power to energize ownership and engagement in the value of service. Top management has the authority to get direct resources, approve specific needs (e.g., training, updated technology), and become the catalyst, the Synergist, the champion, and the chief inspiration officer to team leaders, department heads, and the entire company.

"If the boss takes it seriously, everyone else will!"

Many executive teams I have worked with have displayed remarkable commitment, diligence, integrity, and tenacity. They believe in the value of service as an operational driver and financial strategy. They understand that it's not "just a training program." The rewards have been equal to their commitment. Strategically, it makes sense to take care of the primary revenue source of the business, and when service is done in an exemplary fashion, revenues increase.

Chapter #2: Ensure Executive Commitment and Leadership

Know the Difference between Managing and Leading

There is confusion between the role of managing vs. leading and the concept of management vs. leadership.

- **Management** is about your business systems and processes.
- **Leadership** is about its people.

Yes, we need outstanding systems—but not to the exclusion of the leadership role. You need to be a good manager and create good, workable systems that your team can efficiently apply on a daily basis. As a manager, you can effectively manage systems, processes, schedules, cash flow, and capital. But you cannot be as effective in managing people unless you take off your "manager" hat, put on your "leader" hat, and learn to lead them instead. People are more effective and produce better results when they are led. As a manager, it's much easier to tell people what to do and, if they don't do it, fire them. Easy! But it is different being a leader. Leadership is more difficult than management because it requires an understanding of human behavior.

Yes, effectiveness requires a good system, but a good system is not enough to succeed. If there is no buy-in, negative mindsets will prevail. Your team needs to have the right mindset to engage actively. Providing the necessary motivation, direction, and focus is the responsibility of leadership. You can have great systems, but if you have poor leadership, you will have poor results.

> *"The key is to be a good manager and a good leader, not one or the other."*

For transformational processes, such as creating "WOW" Factor! experiences, you need to place more emphasis on leading and directing the team toward the goal. It isn't easy to follow someone who is standing at the back of the team, pointing to the front and yelling out which direction to take. That isn't leading or delegating—it's abdicating your responsibility and role as a manager and leader.

As a leader, it is your job to coach, teach, and build high-performance teams. You will not get the performance you are looking for using "control and command" management methods. Leading means you are responsible for the success of those you are leading. You cannot exclude yourself and lay blame at the feet of your team. When you are a leader, the buck stops with you. This is not easy, but it is highly effective in increasing productivity and performance.

Good leadership produces willing participation. As a result, attrition reduces dramatically, costs come down, and people do not shoot each other!

Chapter #2: Ensure Executive Commitment and Leadership

Choose Service as a Core Value, Operational Driver, and Financial Strategy

A singular focus on driving the bottom line instead of providing a "WOW" Factor! service temporarily helps an organization cut costs. However, unless this is done wisely, the real costs can be extremely high. Short-term thinking will most certainly do damage to the business and will inhibit future growth and shareholder returns.

How? When your organization is not glued together with a strong set of core values, and you don't have a clearly defined offensive strategy that includes anticipated contingency plans to take advantage of changing market trends, the only option left is defensive-reactive-style decision-making.

This leads to daily, weekly, and monthly panic attacks and irrational premature cuts that erode staff morale, customer confidence, product quality, and, of course, industry reputation and branding. The leadership brand in many industries stinks! You cannot cut staff and programs, such as quality management, sales, marketing, and training, and expect to achieve the same level of success. It's an illusion that has destroyed many great businesses. The answer is to passionately focus on "WOW"ing customers—the revenue source of any business.

The idea of customer service as a value and part of the culture then becomes a much greater concept when you realize that it's as essential to be helpful to your internal customers (your team) as it is to be beneficial to your external customers. We are all customers, and we are all, in one way or another, suppliers, even when there is no trade-off. Directly or indirectly, we supply external customers with services, products, or both. We are all suppliers within our own companies, too. Payroll is a supplier to everyone in the company who draws a paycheck. It supplies services to the whole organization. Top managers supply employees with leadership, training, role modeling, career building, and motivation. No matter where you are in a company, no matter your job description, you are a customer and a supplier to others in the company.

For sales representatives and managers, knowing that you need to provide excellent service to your internal customers gives you an important reason to avoid promising your external customers more than the rest of the company can deliver. For instance, when you promise a customer fabulous discounts for a top product that will be delivered in no time at all, this promise will come back to haunt those in Production, Shipping, and Accounts Receivable.

In the end, if your internal customer service is lacking, something is going to give. So, what will it be? Most likely, speed, responsiveness, motivation, team spirit, and/or great talent won't stick around because trying to meet impossible demands makes the work environment unbalanced or toxic. The ultimate result of your promise is an external customer who is unsatisfied, angry, and disappointed, and internal customers who are stressed out by trying to meet compounded unreasonable demands. It's no surprise that maintaining good internal customer relations is one of the key success factors required to build trust, which will go a long way toward "WOW"ing your customers.

In the many companies I've worked with, positive human interaction, recognition, and a sense of belonging have always been the major motivators and operational driving forces. As one shop floor team leader explained, "When we trust one another and attitudes are positive, and we feel safe, it's fun to come to work. The willingness to work together to serve customers or to be involved in change programs such as Six Sigma, ISO, or the Synergy "WOW" Factor! is easier, and we give of ourselves without hesitation."

Start the "WOW" Initiative with a Clear Picture of the Destination

A vision is a clearly defined mind image of what the final picture of success looks like. It's a uniquely human ability to imagine and visualize in detail where we plan to end up. To visualize is the most powerful ability we have. When we focus on a specific vision and we discipline ourselves to hold an image constantly in our minds, these images influence our emotions (motivation is an emotion). Our emotions then energize us to bring about the vision's physical materialization.

> *"Imagination is the source of possibility and the foundation of probability. It is the playground of potential, where the seeds of greatness are sown, and the power of belief begins"*

We draw great inspiration every day from the heroes of imagination who have come from every walk of life. The Wright Brothers, George Washington Carver, Albert Einstein, Harriet Tubman, Thomas Edison, Ada Lovelace, Nikola Tesla, Alexander Flemming, and more recently, Steve Jobs, Jane Goodall, Barrack Obama, Kalpana Chawla, Jeff Bezos, and Elon Musk imagined radios, televisions, telephones, computers, incandescent light bulbs, automobiles, aircraft, highways, spacecraft, the internet and a better future for all. Like Martin Luther King Jr., most of them were incorrectly told to stop dreaming about the impossible. Their dreams have proven stronger than the doubters—turning the impossible into reality.

> *"Dreams are always more powerful than the impossible"*

Once, when I was flying to present my synergistic ideas to a group in Orlando, Florida, I looked out on the runway. I found myself staring at a Boeing 747. At such close proximity, the size of it was overwhelming. I was absolutely "WOW"ed by the magnificence of this man-made flying machine. It reminded me of how

Chapter #2: Ensure Executive Commitment and Leadership

far we have come technologically. We have conquered the skies—and it all began with a dream, a vision.

The Wright Brothers had a dream that one day they would fly. Strangely, their father, who was a preacher, had once commented, "If God wanted man to fly, He would have given him wings."

Well, little did Pastor Wright know, but God had given his sons the very wings they needed to fly. Nobody told the Wright brothers they couldn't do it, so they dreamed the impossible dream and turned the vision into reality. That was a great gift to humankind. It began a wonderful new world that started a never-ending, exciting, and adventurous journey from walking on the Moon to probes on Mars . . . and we've only just begun.

Amazing things materialize when the imagination is allowed to play, create, and connect with all other knowledge in the universe.

Dreams have a way of igniting other people's interest, and before you know it, teams of people work in harmony and create greater and greater synergistic achievements.

Writing out a vision statement of what you want your company or team to achieve will ignite this greatest human capability of all . . . imagination, which is the workshop of the mind. Out of that workshop, a picture can manifest into a zone of inspiration, which is where the seeds of greatness are planted.

> *"As a man thinketh in his heart, so is he."*
> -The Bible, Proverbs 23:7.

Realistic dreaming is an integral part of getting a clear picture of your destination so you can create a customer focused plan.

Equally as important as the vision are the supporting values and goals. Core values form the foundation, behavior, and personality of a business. They need to be part of the destination, too! Core values define and guide the business, allowing employees to identify with the purpose—what it stands for and, in this case, why service is a valuable driving force. Values create the platform for people and teams to communicate with one another and understand how they build organizational culture. When values are chosen wisely and practiced diligently, a climate of trustworthiness is built between management and staff. This inspires willing attitudes and teamwork that, of course, ripples out to the customer.

A good customer-focused plan recognizes that a high-performance team culture incorporates these core values, which is a distinct and powerful competitive advantage.

The business world thrives on high energy, enthusiasm, ideas, and innovation. While ideas and innovation are the lifeblood of business, execution, and achievement of goals are the energy source.

Without a clear picture of the destination and clearly defined, written-out, step-by-step goals for how to reach this destination, a business runs out of gas. New products, solutions, concepts, and the best, most well-intentioned plans will consistently fail without vision, values, accountability, and goals. A key to making all this happen is to create a psychology of shared destiny.

Understand that you are in the Business of Directing Energy

"Alice: Would you tell me, please, which way I ought to go from here?

The Cheshire Cat: That depends a good deal on where you want to get to.

Alice: I don't much care where.

The Cheshire Cat: Then it doesn't much matter which way you go.

Alice: ...So long as I get somewhere.

The Cheshire Cat: Oh, you're sure to do that, if only you walk long enough."

-Lewis Carroll, *Alice in Wonderland*

We are all in the people business, and we need to think about what we're doing to direct the energy of these people. High productivity and extraordinary performance are directly connected to how human communication and energy are directed. If our energy is directed toward "WOW"ing the customer, it opens fresh new ways of thinking. When we deliberately and purposefully engage customers, it's all about satisfying their needs and wants and creating trust so that cooperation grows and success is inevitable. It's all about the experience!

> *"It's Ready, Aim, Fire . . . Not Ready, Fire, Aim!"*

Create a Psychology of Shared Destiny

Psychology of shared destiny - in this case, the shared destiny of creating an internal culture of service that enables the entire team to "WOW" customers with ease - is a power source for growth and profitability. Being able to direct energy toward this shared destiny is both an essential piece of the success puzzle and a powerful financial engine. As doing so requires trust between the executive team and the rest of the organization, trust is without question one of the key ingredients to companywide team engagement.

It is leadership and management's responsibility to inspire and empower everyone to share in a common vision, a clear set of values, and clearly defined goals. This can be a very difficult thing to accomplish because many leaders are stuck with a false idea of power and control. Imagined power and control can be very intoxicating and difficult to let go of. After

Chapter #2: Ensure Executive Commitment and Leadership

all, "it's good to be king!" To be feared! This way of being the "king" feeds the ego and creates an illusion of power.

It takes a real shift in thinking, strength of character, and personal confidence in one's own ability to recognize that true leadership power is earned through authentic command presence, honesty, competency, trust, and respect. You cannot lead others if you cannot lead yourself. You cannot build teams if you're not a team player. You cannot create a psychology of shared destiny if you're coming from the wrong place.

You have to trust yourself enough to trust others. In trusting others, you free them up to perform to their highest potential. This is a more successful way to be king! People love to work for and support secure leaders and be a part of high-energy organizations that allow them to grow and develop.

Most people will not align themselves with bad business practices, executive greed, exploitation, verbal and emotional abuse, betrayal, or false promises. Avoid the mistake of thinking that employees will wholly support any of these unethical practices under the disguise of being a team player.

Most people can read between the lines; they share thoughts, assumptions, and information at the speed of the Internet. In today's businesses, good, bad, assumed, and created news travels really fast. That's why constant and transparent information sharing is critical and vital to organizational change. When facilitating change you should follow a set of ethical principles to build a bridge of trustworthiness for employees to walk over without fear.

Make your service culture a manifestation of a shared destiny. Enthusiasm and inspiration are contagious and attractive. Human connection is a primal need. When we connect in positive ways and work together toward a shared destiny, we experience a deep primal validation and a sense of belonging, which results in an emotionally secure workplace—a place of safety, trust, a sense of balance, and certainty.

Make your Culture a Competitive Advantage

Building a strong service-oriented organizational culture has immense and profound strategic advantages. Once established, a strong culture made up of solid work ethics, respectful communications, and quality workmanship will create a self-monitoring, consistent, secure, high-performance team.

A stable workforce, where the relationships at all levels of the organization are based on agreed values, has a willing and greater commitment, less attrition, less conflict, fewer politics, and less financial exposure. A culture that creates this is a significant competitive advantage.

As a general rule, people don't sue people they like. One of the most powerful human motivators is a sense of belonging. When we feel we belong, it is a validation of our existence. We will go to extraordinary lengths to protect who we are. Our culture helps to explain our identity and gives us our uniqueness, which we will fight to protect. This, on its own, should be enough to convince the most ardent cynic that organizational culture is a valuable human motivator.

> *"Technology > Synergy > Transparency"*

Understand your Organizational Structure's Effect on Exceeding Customer Expectations

You may not realize it, but your organizational structure will have a direct impact on your ability to create Synergy "WOW" Factor! service.

The "Control and Command" Structure

Control and command structures are the oldest organizational structures on earth. They were originally used by armies to organize and mobilize troops and logistics. These structures are top-down and are designed to control decisions and maintain and concentrate power at the top.

As organizational structures, they were successful in their time. They were employed to build the Pyramids, the Parthenon, the Great Wall of China, and the Roman Empire. As we study business history, we notice many great things were achieved through these organizational structures. For example, during the Industrial Revolution, these structures prevailed and were embraced by industrialists. They worked well in an age where labor was plentiful, the few ruled, and the many were "beholden" to them.

As the Industrial Revolution progressed and factories became more mechanized and geographically spread out, more people needed to be educated to fill the needs of progress. The advocates of control and command were naturally uneasy about letting go; they wanted to maintain power. However, times were changing rapidly. To remain competitive, power needed to flow downward.

The "Competitive" Structure

"Business birth is very intoxicating, and power is difficult to give up!"

Multinational markets forced thinking to change, and a flatter structure was born. To maintain control, the culture and systems became more regulated, with stringent rules and harsher consequences that made workplaces competitive and fearful. A focus on short-term results and a strict adherence to quarterly budgetary compliance became the new way of maintaining power and a determining factor as to whether you kept your job or not. Internal competitiveness became the new method of control.

Internal competition dissipates energy and puts the focus largely on each other, rather than the organization's overall goal. It creates an uneasy, insecure environment that breeds fear, hostility, and a high degree of backstabbing. At the same time, that fear also creates a sense of urgency. Things get done quickly, mostly to ensure job security. Unfortunately, the threat of being fired affects the quality of work, and costs run much higher. Loyalty to the customer takes on a less important role; real loyalty is virtually nonexistent, and litigation costs escalate!

That said, competitive structures do have redeeming qualities. If you are talented and mentally tough, you can move up through the organization quickly and be rewarded quite handsomely. But, as many executives have discovered, these are mostly short-term gains and the hammer can come down rather quickly.

Competitive structures, like traditional control and command structures, demand that the employee focus on the boss and the data. This sets the standards: Fear the boss! Fear the data! The boss gets all the attention, and employees compete to gain recognition. They jockey for office and company function positioning. I have seen the emotional impact of this style on junior employees. Their days are either up or down, depending on a simple acknowledgment from the boss. Needless to say, this is a highly political environment. If you are a good game player, you do well. If not, you suffer.

Recognize that Today's Workers are Demanding Change

The underlying assumption made by the proponents of both the control and command and the competitive structure is that, at some level, people are not smart enough, are inherently lazy, dislike work, and therefore, need to be supervised with a high level of control (McGregor's Theory X). During the Industrial Revolution, that worked well because society was more conformist, and citizens and families were controlled through patriarchal, religious, political, and bureaucratic rules, regulations, and norms. But these structures are now obsolete.

The interesting change that has come about in the last fifteen years—but even more so recently—is the recognition that these structures are as outdated as the technology of the past. Today's workers are demanding a new workplace, a different way of working together. There is a social revolution happening. A critical mass of younger employees are looking for a change from the old way of doing things to new ways in which they can belong and contribute. The majority of those in the Gen X, Millennial, Gen Y, and Centennial (Gen Z) generations want a greater say in the things that affect them. They want meaningful work that has a sense of purpose. They don't want and will not tolerate the old top-down styles of management. They simply will not work for them. They are comfortable with change, want change, and want to be a part of creating the future. They are excited by technology, cooperation, and the loyalty of relationships, and they want leaders they can learn from and admire.

The change that is wanted is a collaborative effort with a focus on a value-driven, shared destiny. The Internet and all its communication speed and the sharing of ideas is a huge synergistic structure that connects anyone to everyone. AI, Google, LinkedIn, and Facebook are the new avenues of business communication and social interaction.

The "Synergistic" Structure

Companies that have synergistic organizational structures lead with a clearly defined vision, a clear set of goals, core values, and purpose-driven leaders who believe that value-driven organizations will always be more successful in the long term.

For years, I have known that the most successful businesses were all about alignment, integration, and integrity and that their leaders were the opposite of the hyped-up image of those portrayed by the media.

Some years ago, I received a copy of Jim Collins' *Good to Great* book. As I read his empirical research on Level 5 Leadership, my years of coaching experience and knowledge about what made a successful leader were validated. What a great day that was!

> *"We were surprised, shocked really, to discover the type of leadership required for turning a good company into a great one. Compared to high-profile leaders with big personalities who make headlines and become celebrities, the good-to-great leaders seem to have come from Mars. Self-effacing, quiet, reserved, and even shy, these leaders are a paradoxical blend of personal humility and professional will. They are more like Lincoln and Socrates than Patton or Caesar."*
>
> *- Jim Collins, Good to Great*

In all the successful companies I have worked with, leadership is encouraged at all levels of the organization, and empowerment is seen as a strategic advantage rather than a loss of power. Synergistic organizational structures attract talented individuals who see that the leadership culture and structure, allow them the opportunity to grow and develop. They are secure within themselves and are willing to work with and share knowledge with other secure individuals.

The leaders who implement synergistic structures are passionate about their work and see work as fun, exhilarating, and "can't-wait-to-get-started." Synergistic leaders are acutely aware of what Buckminster Fuller said: "Real wealth is knowing how to direct energy". Human beings are best when they are relaxed and feel a sense of belonging, regardless of gender, race, age, size, religious beliefs, etc.

When an organization has a synergistic structure and culture, change becomes a source of strength rather than a source of stress. You are part of a high-performance team. High-performance teamwork is demanding and difficult. Each person must be trusted to perform in a responsible, reliable, and responsive way. It's a self-policing system with no place to hide, where everybody is trusted to do their best. If they don't, the team will let them go. The most profitable companies in a variety of industries employ synergistic structures of one kind or another, including Southwest Airlines, Nestlé, Ritz-Carlton, SpaceX, NASA, Amazon, Google, Starbucks, and Facebook, to name just a few.

Synergy "WOW" Factor!

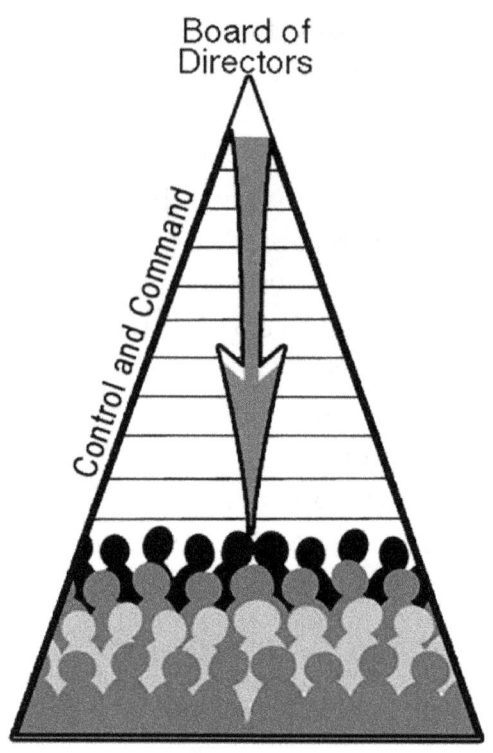

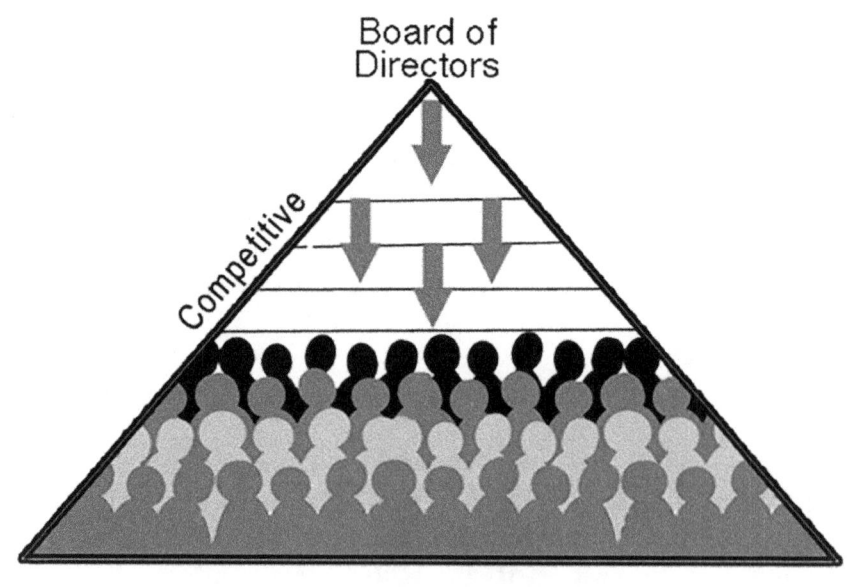

Chapter #2: Ensure Executive Commitment and Leadership

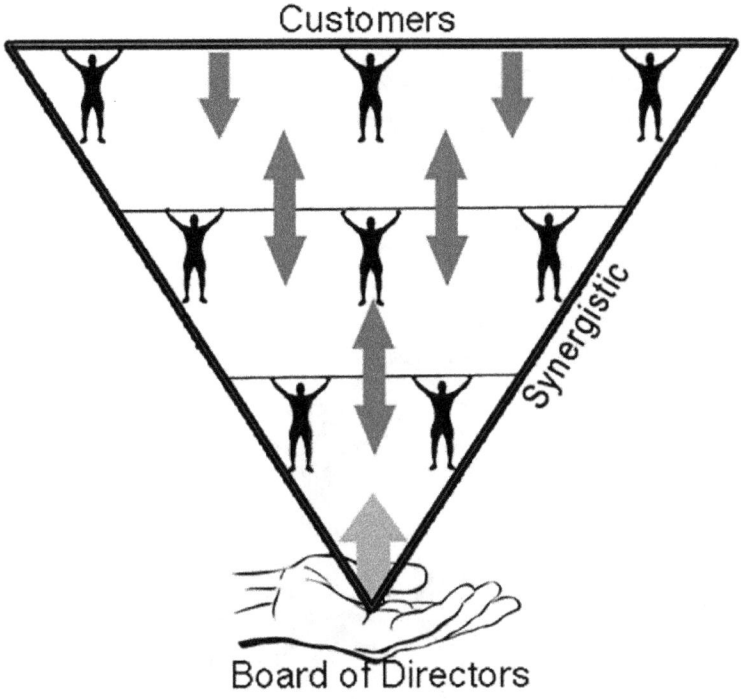

"A practiced value, like "WOW" Factor! service, is a declaration of your integrity"

Chapter Three: Create Goals and a Plan to Deliver "WOW" Experiences

The days of making customers jump through hoops are over. Involving and empowering operational leaders and influencers to embrace service as a major driving force will be the greatest influence of ownership to a shared destiny. This, in turn, will build a powerful synergy of people, systems, and processes at all levels of the organization.

In many ways, creating "WOW" Factor! customer experiences are like orchestrating and writing a symphony of operational excellence. It begins with creative composition and vision, which then must be

Synergy "WOW" Factor!

manifested into a written theme. You can think of every person in the company as an orchestra member. Just as creating beautiful music requires each musician to play their part with precision and harmony, delivering a "WOW" Factor! customer experience depends on every team member clearly understanding their role in the symphony. It's this synergy that transforms ordinary moments into extraordinary ones—exciting, delighting, and truly "WOW"ing our customers. Key leaders and divisional heads must orchestrate, conduct, and align their business sections to the theme, to perform a symphony of operational excellence. When there is alignment, and everyone is playing from the same sheet of music, the customer receives the most efficient service possible, regardless of department or request.

"Passion infused into the right musical notes always exhilarates the audience!"

Chapter #3: Create Goals and a Plan to Deliver "WOW" Experiences

Choose a Theme and Goal that Tie Together

If you want to materialize "WOW" experiences daily, you must establish specific execution goals. Your team needs to have a clear direction and focus to deliver effectively. People follow leaders who are confident and sure about the journey ahead.

A Synergy "WOW" Factor! goal is ambitious, challenging, and companywide. It gives everyone goosebumps at the very thought of achieving it. It needs to make everyone say, "Oh, WOW! That would be great!" In addition, it must carry a message that drives, promotes, advertises, and energizes with the same vigor used to launch a leading product. In fact, one can liken the "WOW" Factor! goal to a major product launch, in which service is seen as equal to and as valuable as the products you sell.

Using a theme name linked to your Synergy "WOW" Factor! goals is an excellent way for your team to get behind the behaviors and actions needed to deliver "WOW" experiences. The whole team should choose the theme name which can be used as a fun buy-in exercise. Communication from the CEO should be rolled out companywide as a bottom-up process, empowering and engaging as many people as possible. This will create a critical mass of ownership and synergize the program.

Some great slogans can materialize from this shared destiny exercise. Examples of these names are:

- The "Oh WOW" Program
- "WOW"–Wonderful Outstanding Workers
- Be the Difference
- Going Beyond, Creating Value
- Made to Inspire
- Exceeding Customer Expectations

Several companies I have worked with have preferred not to use a theme name but rather use their core values as the link for reinforcing the customer's "WOW" experience.

Create Specific Goals for each Team Member

Once you have identified the overall goal and theme for the company, you need to break it down so that each member of your "orchestra" is given a part to play. In other words, you must create clearly defined goals for each team member as a manifestation of your theme. For example, a Customer Service Manager (CSM) could ask the team's individual Customer Service Representatives, (CSR) "What three goals can you individually set in your daily work as a CSR that will make customers say, *Oh "WOW!"*? The same could then be asked of the CSM, and so on.

Chapter #3: Create Goals and a Plan to Deliver "WOW" Experiences

A good plan connects personal and company goals and effectively directs energy toward them. To power up the motivation and commitment, align the customer experience and team behavior goals with personal goals. If you find out what your team members want (their hot buttons) and help them practice the Synergy "WOW" Factor! Principle #3 (Living and Working with Purpose); it is easier to set and achieve personal goals while also achieving "WOW" goals. For example, if a team member wants to buy a new house or give their kids a great education—and you can help them see that those things are attainable—then personal motivation and commitment will follow as surely as day follows night.

In this way, the companywide Synergy "WOW" Factor! goal is communicated, understood, and implemented by everyone through their individual smaller Synergy "WOW" Factor! goals. These are set at every level according to the person's specific department, job function, or position. All Synergy "WOW" Factor! goals are aligned and integrated into the company's overall strategy, mission, and core values.

When you take this approach, you'll find that clearly defined measurements of performance, corrective action steps, and continuous improvement become a 1+1=3 force multiplier. A passionate leadership focus and commitment from your strongest and most committed team players will energize the rest of the team, creating a critical mass of ownership, which will make it happen.

Ensure your Goals have these Characteristics

To increase your chances of success, each goal must:

- have a time limit
- be realistic and challenging
- be written down in detail
- be clearly communicated
- be aligned to the vision, values, mission and measured regularly

Have a time limit: Time limits are important because they create a sense of urgency and neutralize the thief of time: procrastination. A do-it-now mentality creates the right motivational tension. The right amount of tension directs energy, excitement, and focus, leading to consistently satisfying results from individuals, teams, and the company.

"Timing is everything!"

Be realistic and challenging: If you set unrealistic goals, you will de-motivate your team, thus turning tension into demobilizing stress and creating a culture of stagnation (nothing seems to take off). Great care must be taken to set achievable goals with the right amount of stretch, to create the belief of achievability, enthusiasm, and tension to make it happen. As realistic goals are achieved, confidence grows, and your team will willingly reset continuous incremental sub-goals.

Chapter #3: Create Goals and a Plan to Deliver "WOW" Experiences

As each sub-goal is achieved, confidence grows even more. I have seen this prudent and patient strategy achieve success over and over. Increasing sales by 2%, for example, is completely possible and bearable and can be accomplished easily and regularly. You achieve extraordinary results by using the power of compounding growth and motivational intelligence. A 2% monthly increase in most businesses is quite acceptable and possible. Two percent compounded is an annual increase of 26.82%!

Be written down in detail: Written goals take on greater intensity because of the clarity of expectations. Written goals will narrow down the focus to relevant issues and activities and become a platform for ongoing communication to redirect and reward efforts and achievements.

Be clearly communicated: Communicating organizational expectations and team expectations cannot be overemphasized. In all the companies I've worked with, the one common area that has consistently created conflict, misunderstanding, dismissal, and lawsuits is the lack of importance placed on proactive communications and clearly detailed expectations.

Be aligned to the vision, values, mission and measured regularly: As with the vision and values, goal ownership will strengthen the potential for success. Goal alignment, however, should include a coaching and training session on how individuals can achieve their personal goals through achieving company goals.

This is where synergism can take a firm hold. When you show someone how they can fulfill their dreams, you win their hearts and minds instantly. When a leadership team takes the time to establish the key motivational hot buttons of individual employees, it energizes a power source, leading to inevitable success. This is what Buckminster Fuller meant when he said: *"Real wealth is knowing how to direct energy."*

Think World-Class

When you think world-class, you automatically feel and behave differently. To use a sporting analogy: There are club games. There are statewide games. And then there are national and international playoffs. When you represent your club, you have a club state of mind. When you represent your state, you have an elevated state of mind. But when you are representing your country at the Olympics, your mental, emotional, physical, and spiritual energy becomes more intense, focused, and concentrated, resulting in shattered world records and the wildest of dreams being fulfilled.

It is not just the winners affected by the vision and passion; everyone touched by it grows. To a person, every Olympian, coach, trainer, parent, sibling and supporter is inspired and moved by it. Why should it be different in business? Indeed, many inspiring rags-to-riches stories have caught our imagination, and we can draw ways to become world-class from them.

Chapter #3:   Create Goals and a Plan to Deliver "WOW" Experiences

In the context of "WOW"ing customers and building an organization that delivers world-class service, the vision needs to be "world-class." World-class service is experienced by customers dealing with an organization that chose to be in integrity and foster transparency; clearly living out a set of core values as guiding principles focused on creating "WOW" experiences as a declaration of trustworthiness.

Think in terms of having a world-class vision of the "WOW" Factor! service and then create a plan to make it happen.

I once had a terrible experience at a hotel that clearly was not thinking world-class.

It was 10:00 p.m., when I finally arrived in Las Vegas. Normally, it's a five-hour drive from Orange County, California, to Las Vegas, Nevada, but not this time! It took seven grueling hours through driving rain and snowstorms. Hungry, tired, cold, and ready to get into my pre-booked, prepaid room. I self-parked and walked the half marathon to the registration desk.

I was greeted by a line of 20 to 30 similarly red-eyed, tired, and frustrated people who seemed bewildered and confused. I soon understood why.

This was the first hotel ever—and I've been in a few—to force their guests to check themselves in on a computer. This is the same self-check-in process used at airports, except there's one big difference:

At airports, they give the tired, dazed, and confused an option. You can deal with a carbon-based life form or use a computer. The choice is yours. This, however, was not the case at this hotel. And, to pour more fuel on the fire of disgust, the computers did not work.

"You have to swipe the same credit card you booked with," somebody yelled. *"I've tried that, and it doesn't work!"* someone yelled back. We gathered around, trying to do the work we had already paid this hospitality establishment to do. It was like a bad comedy scene from a B-rated movie. *"Who the hell is running this place?"* I heard a woman say as she stormed off. I'm sure she went on to find adequate accommodations at an establishment run by real businesspeople.

Finally, there was a flurry of movement as three check-in agents beckoned us to step forward.

"Next!" Yippee, that's me! After another long shlep, I finally got up to my room. Ahhh, at last! . . . Oh no! The room isn't made up! For a moment, I was stopped in my tracks and knew instantly what the problem was: the management of this hotel did not care about delivering quality service to its guests. It was not a part of their business philosophy. Getting a customer's money in advance and implementing shortsighted cost-cutting was their gig. It was all about greed and not customer satisfaction or integrity.

If this hotel management group had integrity, they would be focused on the customer experience. They would measure and improve all of the service methods,

Chapter #3: Create Goals and a Plan to Deliver "WOW" Experiences

systems, and processes they employed to care for me, their customer, and their revenue source. Clearly, they were not!

Of course, very few people are loyal to this sort of business and the cost of attracting new customers continuously is extremely high, even in Las Vegas. So, who are the Neanderthals running these types of businesses, anyway? What are they thinking? Why are they being allowed to make such fundamentally stupid decisions? Don't they know that they wouldn't have a business without customers? Isn't that Business 101? Maybe they are caught up in those corporate data printouts and have to serve the executive gods in the tower instead of the customer. All I can tell you is I'm never going back and would not be surprised to hear that this hotel went out of business.

Create a Plan

Creating a plan is all about the principle of cause and effect. Great planning is the cause that enables any transformational process to have the greatest and most profound effect. Great customer satisfaction is not attained by luck, chance, or horoscopes. It is in the planning and execution that "WOW" experiences materialize.

Before you move forward, you must clearly understand the size and scope of your goal and determine—with your feet planted solidly on the ground—all the functional steps and resources required to achieve success. In other words, you need to make a plan.

The following tools and guidelines will assist you in doing this.

Start with a SWOT Analysis

	Pro's	Con's
Internal	Strengths	Weaknesses
External	Opportunities	Threats

A SWOT analysis begins realistically measuring Strengths, Weaknesses, Opportunities, and Threats. It balances collective viewpoints and opens up many business areas to scrutiny. A SWOT analysis helps your team avoid the pitfalls that are often overlooked in the planning process. SWOT analysis requires fanatical attention to detail. Clear-headed, precise thinking will assist the smooth execution of your plan. Ask your team *"What-if?"*-questions and scan all high- and low-road possibilities.

Project both positive and negative outcomes by going through the possibilities:

- "What would the impact be on your business, and what would you do?"
- "What would the contingency plan look like if certain things didn't happen?"
- And so on.

Then, when you think you're done, realistically ask the question: *"Have we considered all internal and external factors in our SWOT analysis?"*

This critical and evaluative approach builds a sense of certainty. Plus, it reduces the stress impact of market changes and gives assurance that success is a well-thought-out and planned set of progressive steps toward realizing a worthy goal. Once you have completed your SWOT analysis, reassess your mission and goals before writing up your execution strategy.

Pay Fanatical Attention to Detail

As you are creating your plan, plan to pay fanatical attention to detail. World-class companies practice fanatical attention to detail in product development, creating, managing, and improving systems and processes, and clearly understanding every step of the buying experience. Needless steps are eliminated. Customer satisfaction and responsiveness to requests and complaints are measured, examined, and responded to appropriately through continuous improvement work teams. Ambiguity results in costly overruns!

> *"Fanatical attention to detail is one of the key ingredients in making a customer say "WOW."*

The Walt Disney Company is known for its fanatical attention to detail. Walt Disney was an artist who recognized the importance of detail. Every customer, consciously and/or subconsciously, can tell whether the company cares or not by attention to detail in your product or service. Disney believed there was a right way to do things successfully and that this right way requires attention to each step. Standardizing procedures makes it easy to measure, master, and repeat each step to create a "WOW" experience.

Today, Disney measures customer behavior and responses and adjusts its service accordingly. Disney researchers know how long it takes a guest to eat cotton candy while walking down Main Street at one of its theme parks. Based on this observation, they know exactly where to conveniently place a trash receptacle to discard the depleted cotton candy stick. This makes it less stressful and easier for guests to enjoy the Magic Kingdom. It also keeps the park clean.

Disney researchers have carefully selected picture-perfect spots throughout the park, knowing that guests will want to capture and share their experience.

Chapter #3: Create Goals and a Plan to Deliver "WOW" Experiences

Each location is designed to ensure every photo looks flawless—turning every snapshot into a mini-brochure that reflects the magic of Disney.

Disney is not the only company that has discovered that attention to detail pays outstanding dividends. Many companies employ continuous improvement processes to reduce margins of error and move closer and closer to perfection—and it pays handsomely.

The Ritz-Carlton provides another excellent example of fanatical attention to detail. The hospitality industry is brutally competitive. When customers pay hundreds of dollars a night, impeccable customer service is demanded. There are many "WOW" Factor! principles employed by the Ritz-Carlton to ensure you remember your stay, and the Ritz-Carlton remembers you.

The hotel staff is always impeccably dressed in their starched, freshly cleaned uniforms. There are no wrinkled shirts or crookedly creased pants. Why? Because the hotel takes responsibility for uniform maintenance. The uniforms never leave the premises.

The Ritz-Carlton valet is an *undercover agent* for the hotel, he is trained to take notice of items such as drinks and snacks left in the car, he notifies the front desk of the customer's preferances. Guess what happens the next time you arrive? Yep, your favorite drinks and snacks are waiting in your room.

Taking such exceptional care of the customer is not a *"nice-to-have"* in today's competitive environment. It's a requirement.

Achieving world-class customer service is not easy. Getting the customer to say *"WOW"* takes work consistently. It takes a commitment to make service a major operational goal. It must be embraced as a value and it must be measured regularly.

Successfully achieving objectives and goals can be traced back to the organization's quality and planning. Time management, timelines, scheduling, and reporting structure are essential. The leadership group must be able to match talent to function and skills with specific jobs and then form teams of personalities that complement each other.

When it comes to planning, fanatical attention to detail always pays off. The devil is in the details! Checklists, specific methods, and follow-through are of paramount importance. Fanatical attention to detail works extremely well in the franchise, hospitality, health, and entertainment industries and, of course, in aerospace where there is no room for error at all! Doing it right the first time and having zero defects are achieved because of the attention given to organizational detail before and during the execution of the goal.

Chapter #3: Create Goals and a Plan to Deliver "WOW" Experiences

Align your Systems and Processes to your Goal and Culture

You can have extremely talented individuals and teams, but if your systems are poor, you will not achieve the success you envisioned. On the other hand, if you have well-thought-out systems and you back them up with a strong culture and talented individuals working synergistically in teams, you have a winning formula that will make you extremely successful.

The caveat here is that all of your systems must be aligned with your goal and fused with your organization's core values and culture. Making this happen must, therefore, be part of your plan. When this happens, concentrated energy, functions, and systems will be moving in the same direction, creating 1+1=3 . . . or more! When physical, mental, and emotional energy are in sync—supported by a great system and aligned toward a shared destiny—success is a given.

Reward Good Performance

Your plan should make individual performance within the team important, but don't make the mistake of pitting people against each other. Make your teams the heroes of success and reward the performance and behaviors that you want to be repeated. When a particular team does well, bring that whole team in front of the other teams and congratulate them on their great teamwork, spirit, dedication, and commitment to the plan.

When you reward a team with positive reinforcement, they celebrate their success together . . . and repeating good performance becomes easier.

We all want recognition, to know that we're doing a good job and working with great people. Build specific rewards for teams and individuals into your plan to motivate change. Carefully consider financial and personal rewards and make them meaningful.

"If you fail to plan, you plan to fail. If you succeed in planning, you are planning to succeed!"

Align Finance with your Goal

Your financial team needs to be an integral part of your Synergy "WOW" Factor! program. This program is a financial strategy and should be accepted as such.

CFOs and accounting staff often see customer service, marketing, sales, team building, and motivational programs as the *"people's side"* of the business. They think of these things as the "software" (human relations) and not the *"hardware"* (systems and financials) of the business. Financial teams are often excluded from planning meetings based on wrong thinking that customer service training does not

Chapter #3: Create Goals and a Plan to Deliver "WOW" Experiences

affect their job directly. Or that, somehow, customer interaction is secondary to *"more important work."*

All work is important, and all efforts to improve the quality of service are vitally important for both internal and external customers. In the digital world in which we live and work, our customers have many choices—and anyone in any department can push customers away with their attitude. From top management on down, every person in every department is in the service business. Creating "WOW" experiences is an inside-out program with no person or department excluded. The better we serve, the greater the loyalty and referrals we receive. This stabilizes cash flow and dramatically lowers the cost of sales.

Revisit Policies and Procedures

While you are in the midst of creating a plan to reach your Synergy "WOW" Factor! goal, recognize that this may be a perfect time to revisit your policies and standard operating procedures. After all, you may need to change outdated policies and/or procedures to align with your new goal. Review your policies and procedures manuals or consult Human Resources before you begin your new program. You cannot promise things that cannot be delivered because your policies and procedures are antiquated.

For example, for your team members to be able to deliver a "WOW" Factor! service, they often need to be empowered to make decisions on the spot. My colleague Linda's recent experience with the Pacific Symphony in Orange County, CA, illustrates this.

Linda and her husband, Joe, are supporters of the Symphony. Members of the *"Symphony Pass"* donor program are entitled to four free tickets to one of the Symphony's outdoor summer concerts each year. Linda had ordered the tickets and invited another couple to join them for the evening and was getting concerned that no tickets had arrived. So she called the box office and was assured that the tickets would be waiting for her at "Will Call" on the evening of the event.

As it turns out, Linda was right to be concerned. On the day of the event, there were no tickets to be found for them at "Will Call". The CSR checked under Linda's name and checked under her husband's name (they have different last names), but nothing turned up.

Linda politely explained that she was a Symphony Pass member, that these were the four free tickets she was entitled to, and that she had spoken to someone who had assured her that the tickets would be waiting for her. But she had no proof of any of this. No email, no recollection of the name of the person she had spoken to, etc.—and the staff at the venue box office did not appear to have access to the Symphony's computer system.

At this touchpoint, things could have gone very bad. The CSR could have apologized, said there was

Chapter #3: Create Goals and a Plan to Deliver "WOW" Experiences

nothing she could do . . . and lost a donor for the Symphony. But that's not what happened, because the CSR had obviously been empowered to make decisions and take action. Because the concert was not sold out the CSR found four available tickets. "We have upgraded you to a table," she said with a smile as she handed the tickets to Linda.

When Linda, Joe, and their guests arrived at their seats, they discovered they were sitting at a table for four on the grass area directly in front of the stage, two rows back! It was truly a Synergy "WOW" Factor! moment, and they had a delightful evening.

Plan to use Technology to Support and Improve Customer Service

Picture this . . . you call a company whose opening recording is, "Your call is important to us." Then the elevator music comes on, followed by a similar computer voice: "To help you better and more quickly, please tell me why you are calling today." So, you try to tell the computer why you are calling. But because the computer does not understand your accent or your lack of perfect computer diction, the computer voice responds with, "Let's try that another way, shall we?" and gives you a series of options that do not remotely address why you are calling. By now, you're extremely frustrated and quite annoyed about the lousy customer experience.

Once you finally speak to an agent, you find out this is the wrong department and this agent does not deal with your type of issues. This agent transfers you—supposedly—to the right department. Again, the elevator music and long waiting period. When the next agent answers, you must go through all of your identification verification steps before they will discuss the issue. Didn't you already give that information to the previous agent? You still do not know if you have the right person/department to resolve your issue. After that trip through customer service hell, the weirdest thing of all is that you will be asked to rate the lousy service you received.

This entire example is absolutely the wrong way to use the power of technology because it does not improve the experience, it makes it much worse. In fact, it lowers the level of service and damages the customer relationship.

So, why in the world do companies do things this way? Because it's cheaper. The thinking is that it's cheaper, so it must be smarter. Right? Wrong! Just as the United States experienced during the pandemic, cheaper is not smarter. "Cheap" can be very expensive! Perhaps it's also because companies think that the quarterly Earnings Before Interest, Taxes, Depreciation, and Amortization (EBITDA) data and shareholder interests are more important than the customer; or fear runs the business. Then, too, it could be that the company is more tactical than strategic, and therefore indifferent to the broader implications. Or perhaps it is

Chapter #3: Create Goals and a Plan to Deliver "WOW" Experiences

only focused on the short term, with an important contract or executive golden parachute taking precedence. In such cases, cutting costs for short-term gains appears more advantageous.

However, this is not a way to create loyal customers and stabilize cash flow. And it is certainly not the way to create "WOW" Factor! experiences. In every business, customer satisfaction leads to shareholder satisfaction.

All you need to do to lose 1,000 customers today is to have an angry, frustrated customer taking their negative experience to the many social media platforms. In 24 hours, thousands of people will read about it.

So, what should you do? Make sure you deliver on your promises, making the customer the most important person in the business. Do not waste their time and demonstrate a lack of respect. Instead, show respect by being quick and knowledgeable (Principle #6), improving internal and external communication and the quality of the information you share. Technology can be used to help make this happen.

While this takes planning, organization, and training, the benefits will exceed your expectations. This may mean you need to shop for a better phone technology company with more customer-focused and efficient artificial intelligence answering capabilities. You may need to set up your website with a 24/7 chat line that operates in a way that makes it easy to navigate.

Whatever you do, remember that responsiveness is vital, and speed is of the essence if you want to "WOW" your customers. Technology can be a great tool and an outstanding way to support your communication. Align and integrate your technology in every department—interlinking and synergizing schedules, communications, ideas, and customer information. The integration of information is crucial, especially with regard to the experience you create for your customers. Do not use technology for the wrong reasons or in the wrong way (like in the example above).

Technology can help your customers quickly connect with someone who can actually address their needs. Therefore, the other side of this coin must be an overriding commitment to training your staff in product knowledge, problem-solving, teamwork, and interpersonal communication. Many sins can be forgiven if you speak to a knowledgeable individual. When that happens, your customers will perceive greater value in your products and services.

Sometimes technology can also be used to recognize and resolve problems without even involving them. This can create amazing "WOW" experiences for your customers—and this is what once happened to me with Starbucks.

I had emailed a Starbucks gift card to a friend, but he never received it. I discovered that I had sent it to the wrong email address. *"Great, I'll be out $20,"* I thought.

A week later I received an email from Starbucks

Chapter #3: Create Goals and a Plan to Deliver "WOW" Experiences

saying there was an error on the electronic card I had purchased, and they would be re-issuing a new one to me. Five minutes later, I received it. Yowzah! When it came in, I simply sent it on to my colleague. WOW! That was as close to effortless as you can get!

Include your Strategic Alliances and Supply Chain

In today's ever-changing world, strategic partnerships and alliances are critical. When creating your plan, consider the role your outside partners, consultants, and vendors will play in helping achieve your goal.

While supply chains are vital from the services and products standpoint, equally important is the commitment of your supply chain to practice behavioral and quality standards. Include your vendors and supply chain companies in your conference meetings and customer service training workshops. There are many horror stories of trade partners damaging relationships because an organization did not consider the importance of their role in taking care of the organization's customers.

Enjoy a High Return on Investment

In many respects, the "WOW" Factor! is a cultural and financial strategy, not a training program or something nice to do. In many companies that have implemented the "WOW" Factor!, the returns have been nothing short of amazing.

It stands to reason that when systems and processes are aligned, clearly defined expectations are communicated, goals are set, and every department and person is empowered to be a part of a shared destiny. The effect will be spectacular. However, this approach should be seen as being like a long-distance runner, not a sprint. Through great customer experiences, customers become loyal, raving fans and bring in no-cost-of-sale referrals. Depending on the industry, referrals could be a substantial saving of time, money, and human resources.

Chapter #3: Create Goals and a Plan to Deliver "WOW" Experiences

"Loyal customers return for repeat purchases and are inclined to grow with companies they trust and love."

Synergy "WOW" Factor!

"WOW" is all about the experience!

Chapter Four: Implement and Measure Your Plan

"Sell" your Plan to your Internal Team

You've set your goals and made your plan. Now, it's time to implement it!

To successfully implement a major change initiative like the Synergy "WOW" Factor!, all members of your team must understand their functions, what is expected of them, how they will be held accountable, and the company's goals. A conversation about what success looks like is paramount. Explaining how management intends to achieve success will help people connect to what they need to do. The more internal marketing and communication, the better!

You need to *"sell"* your project like you *"sell"* external marketing projects, such as launching a new product. Clear communications and benefits, an outstanding presentation, and enthusiastic, demonstrable ownership will win over the most ardent cynics—lubricate the most difficult plan and make it successful.

Rolling out this internal marketing process is the responsibility of the senior executive and management team. You need to win the hearts and minds of the entire team and get them excited about the entire process. You must sell the theme, get buy-in on the vision, and core values, and commit to the "WOW" Factor! goals.

Hold Regularly Scheduled Synergy Team Power Meetings

Especially if the project or strategic plan involves people from different departments, you will need to hold Synergy Team Power Meetings with the leaders from these departments. These meetings should be focused on setting up cross-functional goals to assist in the execution of the plan at an operational level.

Chapter #4: Implement and Measure your Plan

Remember, what gets measured gets done. Establishing firm follow-up reporting and progress goals and dates is therefore essential. Be careful to set realistic goals that challenge your team while simultaneously building confidence, and then teach everyone to be disciplined and respectful of these reporting dates and agreements.

A project flow chart can be very helpful in setting these progress goals. Flow charts map out the steps of a process so that they can be easily understood and communicated to the implementation team. The benefit of a project flow chart is that the entire team is clear about their role. In the larger context, it also helps each manager, divisional head, and supervisor evaluate and analyze their particular role and how it links into the overall change program.

Using flow charts at the beginning of a change program will enable you to reduce margins of error while also allowing your team to easily and quickly avoid problems by examining if all the steps were included (or taken). If problems arise, flow charts are a great strategic tool that will help you with root-cause analysis to avoid treating symptomatic problems rather than causes.

Flow charts also enhance interdepartmental and functional synergies. Interdepartmental flow charts allow everyone at every level to see and understand their role in the symphony of operational excellence.

Have an "Expectations Meeting" with Each Team Member

Human nature is such that your team members will be more motivated when they know who's in charge and what is expected of them. To communicate this, have an *"expectation meeting"* with each team member. State what you want at this meeting: *"This is what I expect from you."* Then, ask, *"What do you need and expect from me when it comes to supporting you?"* This kind of *"expectations meeting"* fosters healthy, transparent conversation and builds relationship trust.

To avoid misunderstandings and ambiguity, make sure that your communications are very clear and precise and that everybody knows exactly what needs to be done. *"What you expect is what you get."* High expectations will always increase the likelihood of high-performance. The right amount of tension—not stress—directed toward a goal increases human performance dramatically.

Clearly define areas of responsibility and allow your teams to talk through their areas of responsibility so they can better understand how each team member links in and connects to the process.

In 1940, President Franklin D. Roosevelt said that the U.S. needed 50,000 planes a year to win WWII. He expected America to rise to his expectations, and they did. In 1961 President John F. Kennedy announced that we would put a man on the moon within the decade.

He expected this breathtaking goal to fire up the national pride . . . and it did!

At first, these goals were considered too high. Yet, simultaneously, they were clear, exciting, and breathtaking. America achieved both goals grandly. Undoubtedly, their attainment was hastened by the dramatic Presidential announcements and expectations.

That said, you do need to consider if your timing is realistic. Do your team members have the time to make the project a success? If not, revise your timelines and expectations accordingly.

Energize Your Teams

"Train people well enough so they can leave; treat them well enough so they don't want to."
-Richard Branson

Many people perceive going to work as something they *"have to"* do. But whenever you *"have to"* do something, your energy around it is lower and less contagious. Conversely, the members of high-performance business teams *"want to"* come to work every day because it's safe, enjoyable, and rewarding.

"Willingness is a powerful energizer!"

How do you help your team members get to that point of *"I want to"*? You focus on desire motivation, not fear. Trying to motivate people through fear is like putting contaminated gasoline in your car's tank. Your car will run, but it will splutter, run poorly, and cost you a lot of money to run and repair. Desire energy is like high-octane detergent gas and is highly contagious, resulting in extraordinary performance. The key is changing the work perception from *"have-to"* to *"want-to."* This is achieved through a well-structured plan based on leadership commitment, high-performance teamwork, a clearly-defined vision, a set of core values reinforcing the culture, and "WOW" Factor! goals that are measurable, exciting, and achievable.

As the team grows and develops, creativity becomes the by-product. Creative thinking is something team members rediscover as they learn to trust one another. We are born with creativity, but societal pressures force us to focus on logic and conformity. A leader has never created an ounce of intelligence. Leaders can only condition and train the intellect that already exists.

Your job as a leader is to energize people, releasing their creativity and brainpower through synergy and opening your teams up to unlimited possibilities.

As you begin to *"drive"* your "WOW" plan, you will find that people will become more motivated and excited.

As with life, you and your teams will hit roadblocks

Chapter #4: Implement and Measure your Plan

and must take detours. Dealing with roadblocks proactively, in the right frame of mind, is important. Welcome problems. See them as challenges that allow you and your team to learn new ways to succeed. When you are leading a project, you are really selling the vision and the teamwork. You are also asking your team to trust you and your ability to drive the project to a successful outcome. This outcome is what makes the journey stimulating and worthwhile!

Dan, for example, ran into some significant roadblocks almost as soon as he was assigned to lead a team on the assembly floor. With inventories out of control, Dan realized he had to act quickly. The write-offs were excessive and even more difficult to explain. *"Don't people care?"* he thought.

Frustrated over the 75% inventory accuracy, Dan scheduled a team meeting with all the Leads. "*Okay, team, we need to find the missing material. It's out there in the warehouse and is a pain to manage, I understand that, but you are all competent, with years of experience. This is not my responsibility—it is our responsibility, so I trust you will find the material by the end of the day! Let's get it done! Any questions?*" None.

Most of the material was found by the end of the day!

As weeks progressed, there were improvements in communication, dispatching customer orders, restocking returns, and team engagement. While on the floor, one of the assemblers approached Dan and, in a secretive whisper, said, *"I like you."* Of course, Dan was pleased to hear that and asked her why. Her answer made his day. *"You know, before you, we had no clear direction, expectation, or respect for our experience. You gave us that right away! Before you, nobody would bother looking for material. Now, they look."*

Dan had succeeded in energizing his team and was happy on two counts. First, by locating the material, the flow of orders did not stop and start. It was constant. Second, it is always rewarding to allow the talent and competencies of your internal customers to shine. There is always a rippling-out effect!

Help Team Members Shift their Attitudes

Abraham Lincoln wisely said: *"Folks are just about as happy as they make their minds up to be."* When I look at people in my workshops, I search for the fire in their eyes and those who have decided to be happy. Is there an outer reflection of an inner curiosity? I see many willing, *"I'm-ready-to-'WOW'"* eyes, but sadly, I also see many defensive, cold, and *"keep-your-distance"* eyes.

Almost always, those who have *"I'm-ready"* eyes contribute and learn more, have more fun and communicate more effectively.

Resistance is futile. Eventually, the mindsets of those who start with the *"keep-your-distance"* eyes start shifting. When that happens, the magic also happens! Slowly but surely, the eyes soften, become livelier, and start flickering with curiosity. Before too long, thinking has shifted—and once again, I'm stunned by the power of pushing positive energy into a group. It spreads like wildfire!

Hold People Accountable

A great benefit of organizational detail, good planning, and teamwork is that accountability improves. Plus, honest reporting is more accepted and less threatening. Teams hold each other accountable and the peer group pressure creates a greater sense of urgency.

Make *"eliminating excuses"* part of your company culture. When you listen to valid reasons but don't accept excuses, an outstanding thing will happen: Your team will become more self-managing. Each team member becomes more responsible for their actions as they become tuned into reality.

We have all made excuses in our lives (e.g., the traffic, my wife, my dad, my uncle, my aunt, I didn't have enough information, and so on). Competence is the first pillar of real teamwork. Each team member must be efficient at what they do. The second pillar is honesty. If team members are dishonest and make excuses, the team cannot ever trust them completely about anything. When you eliminate excuses and fear, you eliminate interpersonal friction and build a sense of belonging and a source of inspiration. Holding people accountable is key to doing this.

Apply Continuous Improvement

改善 The Japanese principle of Kaizen means continuously improving systems, processes, quality, and performance in every way, every day. It is making small, continuous improvements in many different things—using "baby steps" to cause vast improvements over time.

The Kaizen concept is easy to understand if you remember the movie *"What About Bob"*.

Bob was an extremely neurotic patient whose psychiatrist told him that he could conquer his panic attacks by taking one baby step at a time. He tried it, and it worked. This lighthearted movie reveals a powerful business principle. Once you get your entire team working on continuously improving their jobs, your entire organization will have reinvented itself within a year, and the strategic goals will be achieved.

While applying the principle of continuous improvement, remember that service must be consistent to earn customers' trust. There is nothing more frustrating than inconsistent service. All departments need to be in sync and aligned to ensure the customer has the same "WOW" level of service regardless of who they deal with. The Synergy "WOW" Factor! is effective when different departments buy in and believe they also need to serve internal and external customers. With a lack of consistency, first impressions and good perceptions can be lost. Customers have no idea who or what to believe.

Focus on the Six Most Important Priorities each Day

A corporation president asked a management consultant to help him improve the performance of his top 100 executives. Without hesitation, the consultant said, *"Each day, have them make a things-to-do-today list, and let them try to accomplish the six most important things that must be done today."*

Several months later, the president met with the consultant again and said, *"You never sent me a bill for the last consultation."*

"If it solved the problem, drop a check in the mail that's in direct proportion to its value to you."

Three weeks later, the consultant received a check for $10,000. Fully aware that it's a matter of priority and focus, the consultant knew his advice would work because he had given it to other clients—and it worked every time.

If you do the six most important things in your life every day, you'll accomplish 1,440 in-the-moment, life-changing experiences per year. Now, that's a simple, powerful, and highly effective formula for success!

Watch out for Complacency

Once your organization begins to materialize success, watch out for complacency. The idea that achieving the goal means you have arrived—so you don't have to make the same effort—is very common and your greatest enemy.

"Success can be the enemy of progress"

Make sure that you set your next goal before you achieve your current goal so that you stretch yourself and keep your team excited.

Train your Team to Deliver on your Brand's Promise

"Hire for attitude, train for skills"
-Southwest Airlines

Part of your Synergy "WOW" Factor! plan must ensure you deliver on your brand's promise. After all, you cannot meet and exceed customer expectations if you are not delivering on whatever your marketing materials say your company stands for.

The biggest problem in delivering brand promises is your team! Most employees have not been educated about the brand's meaning and what is required to live up to the brand's promise. This is often seen as

Chapter #4: Implement and Measure your Plan

an advertising line, not a brand promise. However, all "WOW" Factor! goals must include every employee at every level—and training your team to deliver is part of this process. Your entire team should be focusing on actions and behaviors that tie into your brand promise and company values.

When there is a real commitment to doing what your brand says it will do—and that commitment is backed up with visible behavior and actions—you have begun creating customers for life. Delivering on a promise is simply doing what you said you would do. Every time you deliver on a commitment, small or large, you build trust. Ensure that your entire team consistently performs at the level you promised your customers and make every effort to be true to your company's word.

My experience at a local clothing store, illustrates how management's job is to enforce whatever standards the company has set . . . even if doing so may be unpopular.

My niece likes the typical trendy stores. Looking for a gift for her, I went shopping at the local outlet of her favorite clothing chain. A young college-aged manager behind the desk was equipped with a headset for communicating with other associates. As one of the reps came in to start her shift, this manager noticed that she was dressed inappropriately for doing sales on the floor. Her appearance did not meet the brand's promise of what a shopping experience in this store should be like. Instead of ignoring the situation, which she easily could have done, the manager told her to button up her blouse. If necessary, she could buy a new one.

This young manager's actions made a very positive impression on me. He took his responsibility seriously and adhered to the policies laid out by the store, even at the risk of being considered "uncool" by his coworkers. I was so impressed that I called corporate to compliment him, hoping this would earn him some well-deserved recognition.

Make use of Helpful Tools

There are several tools available to assist in tightening up the effectiveness and efficiency of your internal and external customer loyalty levels. These include:

Flow charts. Once again, flow charts offer visual clarity and are advantageous to use as an analysis tool when there is a breakdown in customer satisfaction.

Fishbone diagrams. Cause and Effect diagrams, also known as *"Fishbone"* diagrams, are used in the "WOW" Factor! program to lay out all the steps required to create customers for life. Every department needs to complete a fishbone diagram to help locate internal bottlenecks in services, systems, and policies that may negatively impact the customer experience. Fishbone diagrams can help departments and individuals find ways to smooth up processes. They synergize interdepartmental systems and demonstrate how each person's job is linked to the whole.

Chapter #4: Implement and Measure your Plan

This naturally involves interdepartmental, in-depth discussion, teamwork, and problem-solving. This means that the use of fishbone diagrams also supports employee engagement and breaks down silo mentality and distancing.

Synergy "WOW" Factor! meetings. These meetings are critical to ongoing success. As you plan these meetings, think about where and how your teams will meet. For example, can technology be used cost-effectively to conduct these meetings?

There are 8 major benefits to conducting ongoing meetings:

- Celebrate success.
- Address customer requests and complaints.
- Conduct training and development.
- Have a platform for employee feedback.
- Do team-building exercises.
- Share company information.
- Follow through on goals and core values.
- Apply continuous improvement principles.

Understand that Business Measurement is Essential to Success

"What gets measured gets done"

Plus, without measurement, there is no way of knowing whether you made a good decision. It is through measurement that product quality and service standards are maintained, achieved, and improved. Measurement tools come in many different forms. Total Quality Management, ISO, Six Sigma, and many other systems and processes are tools to measure quality, customer satisfaction, and business efficiency. It is well documented that these processes and measurements reduce costs and increase revenues and customer loyalty.

To avoid being seen by employees as policing tools and/or to avoid the misperception that a good result on an audit means automatic completion, the use of measurements must be well communicated before implementation—including a clear description, intention, and collective goal.

Measure the right things, and you will get the right results. Then, when you feed information back to your teams and reward success, success will repeat itself. Say "WOW" to the world, and the world will say "WOW" to you! It is the law of cause and effect.

Chapter #4: Implement and Measure your Plan

Measure "WOW" Goals, Customer Satisfaction and Loyalty

"Customers do not buy products or services so much as they buy expectations."
-Theodore Levite, *The Marketing Imagination*

Because listening to the voice of the customer and measuring customer loyalty is vital to the success of the "WOW" Factor!, profitability and growth, it should be taken very seriously. Customer loyalty can be directly linked to an increase in revenue and a reduction of advertising costs and cost of sales.

There are many ways to measure customer satisfaction. Here are two ways that are commonly successful:

- In-house rating surveys

- Independent survey companies

Do not assume your customers are completely satisfied just because they're not voicing their displeasure! On more than one occasion, executive teams I've worked with have been shocked by the low ratings they received on their first outside independent survey.

Listening to the voice of the customer can be very difficult because criticism, for many, is a hard pill to swallow. Denial and delusion are rampant, particularly when there is no measurement and accountability. Yet, the very key to success is challenging the status quo and improving on it.

Synergy "WOW" Factor!

Listening to the voice of the customer is actually a critical marketing strategy. Listening, analyzing comprehending, and then responding appropriately is vital. Major marketing awareness plays a key role in your organization's ability to create Synergy "WOW" Factor! experiences.

Remember the days when companies were product-driven rather than market-driven? Well, think about how many of those companies still exist. Of America's 100 largest companies 100 years ago, only ten are still in business.

You are becoming obsolete when you are not listening, adjusting, modifying, and changing. Listening to the voice of the customer can have a significant positive impact on your bottom line. When you are listening carefully to the needs and wants of the customer, understanding their expectations, and exceeding them, you can place a premium on the price of your product.

Olympic champions love measurement, and so do successful businesses. "WOW"ing the customer and loving the idea of measurement is a state of mind. It needs to be done on purpose and with consistency of purpose.

Measure Management and Leadership

Three hundred and sixty degrees (360°) surveys are a way to get feedback on someone's performance from a wide variety of people, including peers, managers, and direct reports. They are extremely effective for analyzing, measuring, and developing executive skills, communication effectiveness, leadership ability, decision-making skills, and team cohesiveness.

The key factors for implementing a 360° feedback survey are:

- Having good preparation
- Selecting the right questions
- Focusing on strengths, not weaknesses
- Focusing on growth, not reprimand
- Including all executives
- Focusing on goals for improvement
- Following up with coaching sessions

Review Employee Performance

Performance reviews can be extremely destructive or constructive, depending on how the process is handled. There is a myriad of negative connotations in the words *"performance reviews."* Perhaps *"personnel appraisal"* would be a better title.

The focus of personnel appraisals should be to:

- Help employees take ownership of the areas in need of improvement
- Build trust through candid and honest leadership coaching
- Set realistic, measurable goals for growth
- Release talent and brainpower

Keep an Eye on Financial Measurement

"Financial measurement is critical to success"

Without cost controls and measures that ensure adequate funds, a business will not survive. Financial measurement data is available daily, weekly, and monthly in most well-run organizations. Speedy and accurate financial information is of enormous value to your organization's strategic and operating plans.

Measure each Salesperson

For many companies, sales projections determine the difference between success and failure. Sales are the lifeblood of any business and its measurement must be taken very seriously.

Chapter #4: Implement and Measure your Plan

You should track and measure the following for each salesperson:

- actual sales volume
- customer loyalty
- teamwork ability
- leadership potential
- drive and determination
- responsibility, reliability and responsiveness
- attitude and initiative
- integrity, honesty and accountability
- product knowledge
- commitment to values/service

Watch out for the High Cost of Poor Managers

Erin was a buyer with a medical company. She regularly discussed scheduling and demands with her director. In a recent discussion, it was discovered that a major supplier, a syringe manufacturer, only had a maximum output of 3,500 syringes per month. Regulatory issues prevented simply bringing on an additional supplier in a short time frame.

During the discussion, it was determined that the demand was for 25,000 syringes by the end of the month. Erin looked like a deer in the headlights. She was dumbfounded. She had not been informed of the massive change.

After the meeting, Erin decided to place a call to the director. While he had only been with the company for a short period of time—about seven months—he was already creating issues within the department. Erin asked the director how long he had been aware of the change. His response was, *"I'm going to throw it back at you. How long have you known you needed the material?"* Then, unbelievably, he hung up.

A short time later, Erin received a callback and an *"apology."* It was an accident. Frustrated with such an attitude, Erin gave the director her perspective on the communication and situation. It was *"unacceptable."*

At this point, Erin was fed up and made an appointment with Human Resources to discuss the director's unprofessional behavior. The hang-up and the lack of communication were both brought up. The Human Resources person sat quietly, taking notes. When the conversation ended, Erin was told that this incident would *"become part of an ongoing investigation."*

This incident is a great example of the behavior of a manager vs. a leader. Obviously, in this case, the director was a manager. When he said, *"Jump,"* he expected you to say, "How high?" Because he was unwilling to accept being challenged, he lost the respect of the team as a whole.

In reality, the leader in this scenario appears to be Erin. Fed up with the director's attitude, she took the only action available. She brought the issue to the attention of Human Resources. Ultimately, she realized she had no control but felt that his days could be numbered because of his short time with the company and the havoc he was responsible for.

An organization cannot afford a poor manager; it can cost the entire team. Is it worth it?

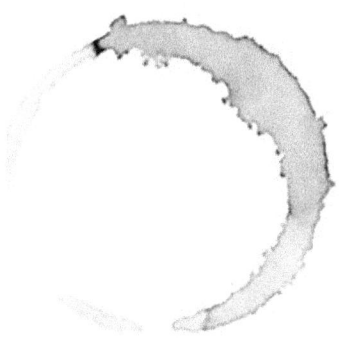

Synergy "WOW" Factor!

Section 3:
Team Members' Role

Synergy "WOW" Factor!

"You cannot consistently exceed expectations if you do not know what your customer expects"

Chapter Five: Manage your Customers' Expectations

First, Understand what your Customer Expects

You cannot consistently exceed expectations if you do not know what your customer expects. Clearly understand what your customer expects so that you can manage and exceed their expectations. If you do not manage customer expectations, they will invent their own.

Managing expectations demands a deeper knowledge of buyer behavior. It begs the question, "What do my customers want?" "What behaviors should I be practicing to exceed their expectations?"

Examples of Customer Expectations	
What do Customers in the New Home Building Industry Expect?	
Product Expectations	High level of quality.
	The expectation is that all the basics need to be in order. The roof does not leak. The doors close perfectly. The plumbing works perfectly. The paint is professionally completed.
Customer Service Expectations for Salesperson and Agent	Educate me on all options available to me.
	Explain the procedure: purchase, loan process, move-in dates, etc..
	Be competent and quick—don't waste my time. I have other models to see.
	Be transparent. Tell me about the problems in the area.
	Tell me about the neighborhood and amenities, schools, and planes.
What do Customers in New and Used Automobile Sales Expect?	
Product Expectations	Stand-by product guarantees and warranties.
	Provide flexible, quick service.
	Have engaging service advisors who don't try to up-sell me.
	Have integrity. Don't talk down to me because I'm a woman.
Salesperson Expectations	Be knowledgeable and personable.
	Show respect. Give me space; don't pressure me the moment I arrive.
	Be transparent. Don't delay details to the end (e.g., interest rates, etc.).
	Do not be pushy and arrogant. Establish my needs.
	Do not low-ball my trade-in. Don't insult me.

There are two basic types of expectations:

- Established expectations and
- Promised expectations.

Address your Customers' Established Expectations

Years of purchasing and interpersonal experiences have established your customers' expectations. All customer expectations are rooted in life experiences, and these experiences are often different in different cultures or societies. For example, in some cultures, demand varies based on the availability of products and services. So, supply drives demand. In the United States and the Western world, the free enterprise system creates greater competition, more choices, and a more discerning consumer. In many ways, demand drives supply. Established expectations are much higher in these countries.

In addition, the Internet has broadened choices worldwide and increased overall expectations. Google's research on purchasing has shown that a potential purchaser will visit many websites before making contact and purchasing a product, all without communicating with a live service agent. Customers quickly learn how to get their needs met. When they don't, they vote with their buying power.

A number of factors related to a person's prior experiences with purchasing, influence their established expectations. Here's how you can exceed established customer expectations and deliver the "WOW" service your customers desire:

Communication: If the communication was bad from just one previous service or product, this is not necessarily your customer's new expectation. However, if they have consistently experienced poor communication from multiple companies in your industry, then that will be what they expect from you. By ramping up your own communications and follow-through, you can set an individual standard that rises above expectations— and results in a stream of referrals.

Respect: You show dignity and respect (Principle #6) by actively listening to your customer's concerns and needs. Do everything you can to put them at ease. Pay attention, make eye contact, and be flexible and approachable. Be aware that being aloof is seen as arrogant and disrespectful in many cultures. Ask open-ended questions to flush out opinions and let the customer know they are important to you. Educate your customers, but do not ever talk down to them. Never make the customer feel stupid or embarrassed about their lack of knowledge—that certainly won't feel respectful! Finally, have a respectful attitude. Later in the book, the importance of attitude is covered in detail.

Responsiveness: Being responsive shows that you appreciate your customer's business and that they are the most important people in your business. Responsiveness demonstrates professionalism and efficiency, two of the key elements of building trust (Principle #5). When a customer arrives at your business, always be the first to greet them and offer your assistance. Do not talk to other staff members as if the customer is not there—show the customer that you are there to respond to their needs, and while you are doing so, nothing else is important.

Value: Is your product or service a good value for the money? Is it worth the price charged? Maybe, and maybe not. The reality is that "value" is a matter of perception. Relationships, branding, and status influence perception. If you are a salesperson, your customer's thoughts regarding your product or service's "value for the money" will depend on many things. This includes their relationship with your company, the quality of the product or service, your skill as a salesperson, the total cost of owning the product, and the status and deliverables concerning the price. The mix of these and other factors, and the relevant importance of each, will vary by market segment. For example, a wealthy executive shopping for a Rolls Royce will perceive what constitutes "value for the money" differently than a recent college graduate shopping for a new Kia.

Efficiency: Few things are as refreshing as discovering a person or company that's truly efficient—what a great day! It reminds me of the old one-liner: Saving you time, saving you money, putting you first! Efficiency talks to many deeper values and demonstrates a well-oiled organization, trained and talented staff, and strong leadership. On a personal level, focus on what you can do to make dealing with your organization as efficient and pleasant as possible for your customers.

Trustworthiness: Trustworthiness is a loaded term and is crucial for developing great internal and external customer relationships. I have never met a person who wants to do business with someone they do not trust. Trusted companies are made up of individuals who demonstrate trustworthiness in their behavior and competency.

Eleven ways to demonstrate you are trustworthy:

1. **Understand that trust begins within you:** All relationships begin with the relationship you have with yourself.

2. **Make the right choices**: No right thing can come from wrong thinking. Be competent at work. You must be trusted to do your part to make the team successful.

3. **Be reliable:** When you say you will do something, keep your word.

4. **Be responsive:** Respond directly to people: Make eye contact and have a firm handshake and good manners.

5. **Be predictably responsible for your actions:** Accept good and bad circumstances and situations. Show your strength of character under adversity. Don't make excuses when you fail—be objective and fix the issue.

6. **Be honest:** Do not embellish, exaggerate, selectively leave out information, or be afraid to express your opinion. Do not lie, cheat, steal, or deceive in any way, for anyone, for any amount of money, or for any other reason.

7. **Be loyal:** Self-serving people are never trusted. Loyalty has a lot to do with trusting yourself and your ability to keep your promises in your personal and business relationships.

8. **Be transparent:** Be open and share yourself to a level of acceptable comfortableness. Politely share your opinions with others. Let people know where you stand.

9. **Be authentic:** False fronts, game-playing, and double standards escalate mistrust and hinder good working relationships.

10. **Admit your mistakes:** Have the courage to admit them, apologize, and move on.

11. **Stand up for what's right:** It's not who's right that counts; it's what's the right thing to do. This is true for all of life's situations.

Synergy "WOW" Factor!

Address your Customers' Promised Expectations

*"One of the most common customer complaints
is that companies break their promises.
In the home building industry, it's all about completion
and move-in dates not being kept;
in the auto industry, it's shoddy service and reliability;
in the movie business, it's all the advertising
hype not matching the delivery."*
The Forum Corporation

If you want to make your customers happy in this area, it's all about delivering on the promise. Eager-to-please or inexperienced customer service representatives often over-promise and under-deliver, leaving customers frustrated and angry. Delivering on the promise carries with it a powerful ethical responsibility.

- What does your company say on its website and in its brochures about what it can do for its customers?

- Does it deliver on that commitment?

If it is an empty promise, then it has no power and it is seen as such by customers.

Staples, the office supply store, introduced a simply brilliant and profoundly important marketing tool: the "easy button," which suggests that purchases are easy, unencumbered, and emotionally and physically safer. This is the promised expectation that their team members must meet.

You, just like Staples, must deliver on your promises! As it is with all relationships, the relationship you have with your customers rests squarely on expectations.

When promises are made and not kept, trust erodes rapidly. The cost is enormous.

The formula is simple: Be smart about making realistic promises and then keep these promises. Do what you say you are going to do! Under-promise and over-deliver, which means you use common sense as your guide. For example, allow additional time for unforeseen circumstances when committing to a delivery date. It is common sense to recognize that things may not go smoothly. To make the customer say "WOW," consider all possible roadblocks and calculate enough time to take care of them. With this approach, you can deliver either early or on time every time.

> *"Consistency creates trust, and trust leads to loyalty"*

In other words, manage expectations by allowing yourself the extra time needed to deliver on time every time. Normally, expectations are created at some interactive point during the transaction. Always allow yourself to be seen as a reliable, responsible person who keeps their word, which builds trust in you and your brand.

This is the way to develop a reputation of "WOW" and a purchasing psychology that is safe and secure for your customer.

> *"Only two percent of unhappy customers complain, while 34 percent penalize the company by switching brands."*
>
> ~A study by AC Nielsen

Be aware of what happens when you over-promise, and understand why you over-promise. Most of the time, CSRs over-promise because they want to please the customer. But in their attempt to do so, anxiety and the fear of loss cause them to make promises they cannot keep. This affects customer trust and, equally devastatingly, can disrupt almost every department in the organization. Consider the high cost of getting it wrong.

Janna's Best Car-Buying Experience

Janna's story illustrates what happens when you meet—and exceed—your customer's expectations... and how sales are lost when you do not.

With close to 150,000 miles on her old car and a promotional email from Mitsubishi, Janna decided it was time to bite the bullet and make a huge investment in a new car. The Mitsubishi was a reliable car. She had had no problems with it at all. The warranty was 100,000 miles, and the service department was excellent. Why not stay with the same brand? She decided to see the new Mitsubishi deals and what they had to offer.

What a difference a person makes. While the Mitsubishi service department was top-ranked, the sales department needed great help.

Chapter #5: Manage Your Customers' Expectations

Janna said: *"It was a week of unnecessary drama! There was an hour's wait at the dealership with no information exchange. A week of daily texts went through without resolution. They didn't want to do a deal but couldn't come right out and say it!"*

The next stop for Janna was the Hyundai dealer. What a difference!

Janna went to the dealership after doing the bulk of the data exchanges through the Internet. She was met by Caitlyn, who had just been promoted from the service department to sales. Her enthusiasm was contagious. It took minutes, not hours, to get the price of a car.

Janna had done her homework by pre-pricing the car at Costco. There was a $500 difference, with Costco being the better deal. Caitlyn price matched, and as an extraordinary "WOW," she added an extra $200 discount. Sure enough, the contract clearly showed the $700 reduction.

Then, the discussion centered on another key factor, the interest rate, which was higher than expected. When the paperwork arrived from the bank, Janna reviewed the figures, pointing out that the contract price was lower. It turned out that the dealership could arrange an interest rate a point lower than quoted. *"Wow, these guys are great!"* Janna thought.

The hour Janna spent at the dealership passed quickly. Caitlyn offered refreshments, and Janna's personal belongings were moved out of her old car and transferred to her new car without Janna lifting a hand. Then Caitlyn did an outstanding run-through of the car's features and a perfect handoff.

Janna said the entire process was *"the best car-buying experience I have ever had!"* The reason why was very simple. Caitlyn understood the value of Janna's time. She had high responsiveness and put the customer first. She was a Sales Hero who was grateful to serve!

As a result, Caitlyn now has a customer for life. Janna commented that there was no one else she would buy a car from due to Caitlyn's attention to detail, responsiveness, and dedication to service. That's what made this the best car sales experience EVER! The voice of the customer was heard loud and clear.

Understand the High Cost of not Living up to your Promises

As Janna's experience with the Mitsubishi dealer illustrates, companies pay a high cost when they do not meet customer expectations. Studies have backed this up. Consider these statistics ...

It's expensive to replace customers: It costs about five times as much to get a new customer as to keep an existing one. It is far better to have loyal customers who love your brand. They are your most precious asset.

Established expectations are low: Four out of five people think product, service, and quality are worsening. Eighty percent of customers will stop buying from a company that doesn't meet their expectations.

Poor service drives people away: Five times as many customers change companies due to poor service and quality, than price.

Poor relationships drive customers away: Seventy percent of customers stop buying because they think the company doesn't care.

Bad attitudes drive customers away: Sixty percent of people who get a positive response when they complain will continue to deal with a company, but 90% of customers will switch suppliers due to negative attitudes and aloof treatment.

Poor responses to problems drive customers away: Fifty percent of people who complain are dissatisfied with their response, and 50% stop buying from the offending firm.

Unhappy customers spread the word: Frustrated customers who use social media can quickly tell thousands of others about their dissatisfaction.

Customers don't always complain: For each complaint you hear, between 20 and 100 go unheard and unreported. These people take their business elsewhere without announcing they are doing so.

The Lennar Corporation: The Synergy "WOW" Factor! in Action

The culture at the Lennar Family of Builders drives performance consistency. The foundation of Lennar's culture is to have fun and practice the *"I Care"* culture values. To a traditionalist, Lennar may seem weird, quirky, maybe even strange. They recite poems, wear badges, and have "WOW" for Now" lunches and meetings.

As a past speaker and workshop facilitator at Lennar meetings, I was impressed by the level of personal commitment and involvement throughout the entire corporation.

Their culture is strong and trusting, with a simple but very effective "WOW" for Now" recognition program.

The individuals selected to be recognized demonstrated to fellow associates, customers, or business partners that they practiced the company's *"I Care"* culture values.

Lennar is a highly profitable, value-led organization with high rates on J.D. Power customer satisfaction listings. Once again, a values-led organization roars ahead, demonstrating that teamwork, caring, and having fun in the workplace are powerful and acceptable strategies that work.

Chapter #5: Manage Your Customers' Expectations

Use Customer Touchpoints to Manage and Exceed Customer Expectations

Customer touchpoints are the points of contact you make with your customers, or they make with your company's brand, product, or service, either online or in person. Developing a series of touchpoints allows your team to manage customer experiences and expectations effectively. Remember, you cannot consistently exceed expectations without managing expectations! Service always begins with serving others, and trust results from responsible and consistent service.

Knowing the steps a customer takes to purchase your product or service is the starting point for creating a touchpoint system. Your goal is to have easy steps for your customers and clear touchpoints that are easy for your entire team to practice. Through effective application and measurement of customer touchpoints, you will improve your ability to "WOW" customers more consistently.

Synergy "WOW" Factor!

The Customer Journey of Touchpoints

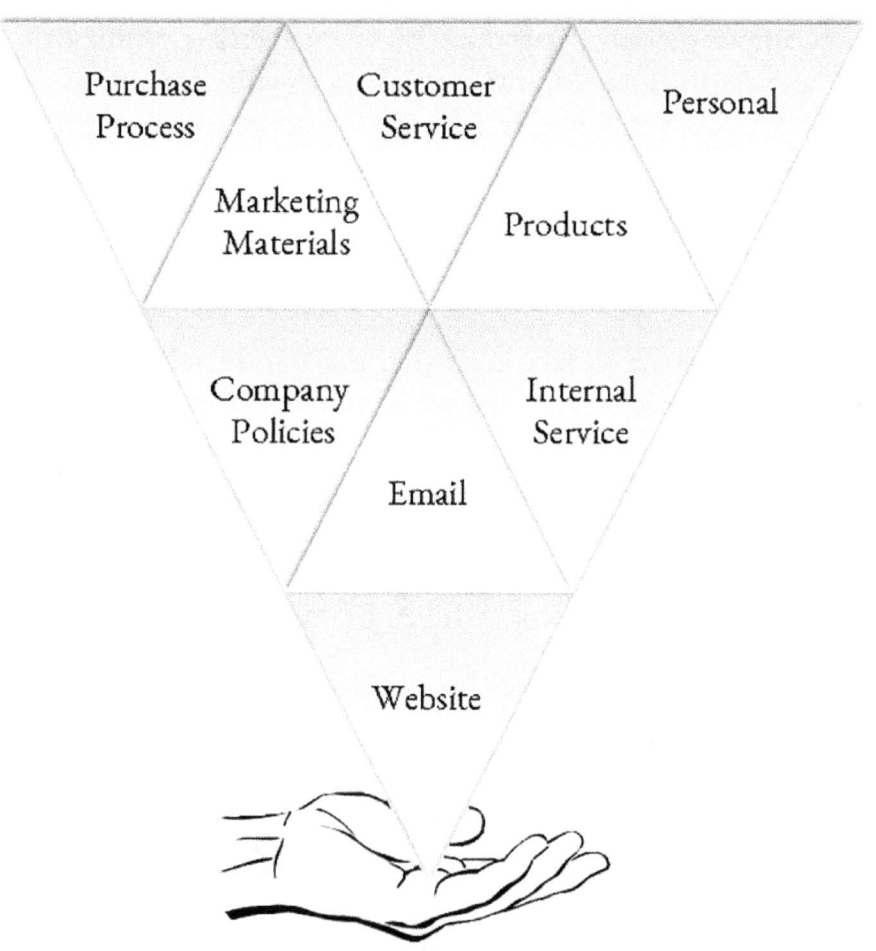

Chapter #5: Manage Your Customers' Expectations

\multicolumn{2}{c}{**An Overview of the Customer Journey**}	
Website	The website needs to be easy to navigate quickly and clearly. Contact information, should be available everywhere.
Email	Observe email etiquette. Use standard English, and don't make the email too long or too short. Practice respect, dignity, and service politeness.
Marketing Materials	Marketing materials need to be clear, professional, and error-free.
Products	Products need to be user-friendly, easy, guaranteed, and high quality. All staff must be familiar with and knowledgeable about the product.
Customer Service	Customer service should always be highly responsive, engaging, professional and intelligent. Problem-solving and all the "WOW" Factor! factors must be in place.
Internal Service	Internal customer service and teamwork need to be highly responsive, seamless, and supportive. No silo mentality, no "this-is-not-my-department" or "I-only-work-here" attitudes. Cross-functional training and teamwork are essential. Customers should be able to transition intelligently from one department to another. Each department needs to address its own set of touchpoints.
Purchase Process	Simplify the purchase process; make it paperless and easy. Reduce the mental and physical effort necessary to complete a purchase . . . the easier, the better.
Company Policies	As they relate to service, company policies can be out of alignment. Re-visit and re-evaluate company policies from a customer perspective, and try to create a triple-win mentality.
Personal	Know your customer demographic and current communication preferences. It is imperative that each person have their own touchpoint method, or each department agrees on department touchpoints.

Understand how Touchpoints Creates the Synergy "WOW" Factor!

Relationships influence perception, perception influences trust, and trust leads to the "WOW" Factor! This means that many customers essentially make decisions based primarily on relationships. It is, therefore, a prudent strategic step to plot out your customers' journey and establish a set of touchpoints that will deliver a "WOW" Factor! experience. Your goal is to create a set of predetermined communications, behaviors, and actions that exceed your customers' current service expectations.

A Customer Touchpoint Example: Hair Salon

The following provides a series of touch-points for a hypothetical walk-in hair salon . . .

Touchpoint #1: The Receptionist's Greeting. Being warmly welcomed into a retail establishment puts customers at ease, making a difference in purchasing decisions. A smile is worth a thousand words! Eye contact and the right mental attitude must be felt, and dignity and respect must be displayed (Synergy "WOW" Factor! Principle #6). Note: See Chapter Nine on Attitude.

Touchpoint #2: The Request for Customer Information. Asking for personal customer information is critical to knowing your customer. However, if done without the personal touch, the customer will push back. This is why staff members need to be trained on how to safely engage when requesting personal information.

Touchpoint #3: The Stylist Introduction. Stylists are artists, and some artists are self-centered. It's all about their work and artistry. If that artistry is coupled with a personal touch, meaning the artist is a respectful communicator, then you have an in-demand service provider whose opinion will be heard. Do not forget Maya Angelou's famous quote: "I've learned that people will forget what you said, people will forget what you did, but people will never forget how you made them feel."

Touchpoint #4: The Consultation. The stylist listens intently to what the customer wants, including any challenges with their hair that they are facing, and then discusses the recommended solution.

Touchpoint #5: The Service. As the person delivering the main service, the stylist has the greatest opportunity to deliver on a promise, exceed expectations, and create a "WOW" Factor! experience. Many of a customer's established expectations will also come into play while they are receiving the main service. Quality is an established expectation aligned with value for money. If a service provider has the whole package, trustworthiness follows along with loyal customers.

Touchpoint #6: The Product Recommendation. While providing the main service, the stylist also has an opportunity to promote a product solution. In this case, it may be a shampoo, conditioner, or other product that will improve or repair damaged hair.

Touchpoint #7: The Farewell. The last and final impression is as important as the first impression. It's all about the experience . . . and we remember experiences. An important part of the farewell at a hair salon is to schedule the next appointment. While the customer is admiring their well-styled hair and basking in the glow of a "WOW" experience you should get their next appointment on their calendar.

> *"First impressions count, but last impressions last!"*

I often think of the similarity of customer service to a stage show. The overarching goal in the entertainment world is to ensure audiences have a great experience. Every story has a beginning, the body of the story, and then, of course, the ending, which makes or breaks the story completely . . . and so it is with service. You should strive to make the end of each service one that leaves the customer being "WOW"ed and wanting more. After a "WOW" experience, customers want their friends and family to have the same experience. Their loyalty to your brand grows, and so do referrals.

Chapter #5: Manage Your Customers' Expectations

Customer touchpoints are critical for ensuring that we give world-class service. As this hair salon example illustrates, if you pay attention to every step of your customer's journey, you will have many opportunities to "WOW" them!

Take Things to the Next Level with Extraordinary Touchpoints

Extraordinary touchpoints are touchpoints that are designed to surprise. They go beyond what's expected and make the customers say, "Oh, WOW! I didn't expect that!" With an extraordinary touchpoint, you provide an unexpected, extra-special event, gift, or service. This completely blows their hair back!

Many companies have discovered the value of surprising customers to lock them in and create memorable experiences. For example...

Apple: In Sydney, Australia, Apple surprised their first eleven iPhone buyers by giving them a standing ovation after they purchased their phones. "WOW"!

Southwest Airlines: Without passengers knowing it, SouthWest arranged for in-flight entertainment by contracting the group "Bare Naked Ladies" to play live while in flight! "WOW"!

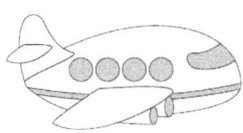

Target: Will Smith and Target got together to surprise customers by having him stream live at the checkout counter at one of Target's stores. Customers arrived to check out, and on a video screen at the checkout counter, Will greeted them and offered to pay for some of their purchases. **"WOW"!**

First Bank: First Bank rewards good customers mostly by surprising them with staff applause.

There are many ways to surprise customers with extraordinary touchpoints. They do not have to be expensive events. In fact, sometimes, a large event can lose its effect because it appears to be too contrived. A surprise could be as simple as a coupon, but it must have a level of real sincerity. "Thank you, Mrs. Smith, for ordering your computer. Since we appreciate you as a customer, please find a gift coupon of $100 toward your next purchase." **"WOW"!**

With a little creativity, you can elevate your customers' experience.

Think about how you can make it joyful!

Deliver Personal "Oh WOW!" Customer Experiences

Creating extraordinary customer experiences is something you can do on an individual level, too. For example, I spoke with one woman who told me about her experience when she finished her final cancer radiation treatment. The technician surprised her by handing her a personalized *"Certificate of Completion"* (an organization-wide extraordinary touchpoint) and singing a heartfelt rendition of "Happy Last Day of Treatment to You" (the technician's own personal extraordinary touchpoint).

Customer touchpoints improve experiences not only with daily purchases but even in the most difficult circumstances.

As a salesperson or CSR, there are many ways that you can make each customer touchpoint a positive experience for your customers, including:

Greet all customers as though they were guests in your home. Set the tone in the first few words. Be respectful, positive, professional, polite, courteous, and efficient.

Take ownership of all customer contacts (e.g., phone, email, text, face-to-face visits, etc.). Avoid all *"stupid talk,"* such as *"That's not my department"* or *"I only work here."* Remember that if and when issues arise, you own the problem until a solution is found. Always ask, *"Is there anything else I can do for you today?"*

- Be responsive. Return customer calls, emails, and texts promptly within the same day. Do not underestimate the human relationship importance of connecting.

- Have a "do it now!" sense of urgency. Address complaints/questions immediately or as soon as possible.

- Always apologize for errors. Never play the **"blame game."** Understand that good recovery from errors will build loyalty.

- Show appreciation. Thank the customer for choosing your company.

- Be knowledgeable, memorable, and proactive.

My Travel Disaster Story:

The world is so small that you can be in another part of the country or even in another country in a few hours. All that is required is to book a ticket, arrive at the airport, clear security, and, hopefully, if all the pieces fall into place, board your plane and arrive at your destination on time.

Unfortunately, the opposite of this nice, rosy picture is often the case. As they say, *"The best-laid plans of mice and men often go astray."*

My airline customer service story did not simply go astray. It was a complete and utter disaster—a horror

Chapter #5: Manage Your Customers' Expectations

story with Southwest Airlines, a company that I know goes to great lengths to take care of its customers.

Here's what happened:

I arrived in Oakland, California, on a Thursday evening, the night before my day-long leadership workshop. Friday went well! The training was highly interactive and fun, achieving the predetermined goal.

Satisfied and feeling good, I returned to the Oakland airport to check-in. Although there were long lines, TSA efficiently moved everyone through security, and I happily made my way to the gate with lots of time for a coffee or some other relaxing beverage.

I sighed and thought I was glad that I would be home at a reasonable time. I texted my wife, "Let's go out for dinner after you picked me up."

I had no sooner sent the text when I looked up and noticed my flight was delayed by an hour. Shortly after that, it was canceled altogether. The flight attendants were gracious, helpful and rerouted many passengers through Denver, Phoenix, and several other airports. I was rerouted to Phoenix; I would be home about two hours later than my original flight. No dinner out! Oh well, some other day!

Ok, I told myself, stay proactive; things like this happen. Yes, it did happen, and it escalated beyond belief.

When we boarded the plane to Phoenix, it all began to fall apart. *"We have a computer glitch, and we've been delayed for take-off; we will let you know as soon as we have more information."*

Finally, after an hour of sitting on the runway, we took off for Phoenix. Because of the one-hour delay, what about connections in Phoenix? There were 140 other passengers, just like me. One hundred and forty loyal Southwest flyers believed deeply that we would each be cared for. However, when we landed in Phoenix, no one was available at the Customer Service desk to take care of us, so we were rushed into the main lobby to be checked into our various flights.

This was not a good sign. I like to read *"Between the Signs."* The second bad sign was the look on the faces of the crew. They were totally unprepared for an onslaught of 140 people who had each intended to fly to a different destination. Panicked and flustered, we were told that the next departure had only 18 available seats. I was one of the lucky ones who got a seat. *"Yes!"* The 18 of us were told to hurry because the flight was boarding. Okay! Then, we were told that we all needed to go through security with our new tickets to be able to board.

Huh? My joy was instantly drained. But, never backing down from a challenge, I said loudly, "Let's go!" Like something out of a comedy movie, 18 of us soon galloped with some heavy luggage, bags of anxiety, and buckets of perspiration.

Phoenix Sky Harbor International Airport is huge,

Chapter #5: Manage Your Customers' Expectations

and time was rapidly slipping. Out of breath, 17 other hopefuls and I, impatient but calm, all smilingly excused our way up to the TSA check-in counter. The friendly but firm TSA security agent immediately said we could not proceed because there was no flight number on our boarding passes. *"Nope, I can't let you through."*

Stunned, we learned that none of us had acceptable boarding passes that would allow us to pass through security because they were not printed boarding passes. The Southwest agent who had handwritten our boarding passes failed to enter the flight number. So, we raced back to the Customer Service desk. Now, feeling as though we were in a tsunami of disorganization, frustration, and anger began to rear their ugly heads, and some of us were extremely loud and colorfully vocal.

*"The 'fun' airline has lost its ****** sense of humor and service . . . and so have I,"* said the young woman next to me.

We got our revised boarding passes, went through security, and returned to the original gate, where we encountered a rather surly agent. This gentleman greeted us with a frustrated, "I was a minute from going home and now I'm stuck… here!" Oh, really?! My sentiments were: You're out of here in an hour and getting paid. None of us wanted to hear it. There was no way of telling how long we would be stuck there. We had missed the flight. We were hungry, thirsty and exhausted. There was no water, and there was no food.

Things quickly went from bad to truly miserable. The surly agent offered us an overnight hotel and the next Orange County departure at 5:30 am—barely four hours later! When details were documented and we arrived at the hotel, there would be no time for sleep. When hotel vouchers are offered to stranded passengers at midnight, it's a red flag. All I could think was, after seeing the first sign, why did I not trust my instincts and rent a car in Oakland? I would have been halfway home.

I was now on a personal quest to get out of Phoenix, but how and when? Enter the day's hero: Maryna, my wife, who found an American Airlines flight to Orange County leaving within an hour. I was booked onto the flight and received a text message from Maryna that said, *"You are coming home, Luvie!"* ♥

A broken-down computer system will prevent any flights from leaving or arriving. With tech issues like this, a lack of control is challenging to accept.

Southwest Airlines has always been known for humor and great customer service. This is why service and individual attitudes are so important. All it takes is one incompetent agent to destroy a reputation.

So, what could this agent and management team have done differently? Southwest could have at least given everyone a bottle of water. If they had any sense, they would have given a voucher to help offset the meal cost. Remember, it's the little things that count. Many small things could have been done that would have

Chapter #5: Manage Your Customers' Expectations

made a huge difference, such as attitude, respect, empathy, and competency.

Having said that, because of Southwest's track record of service with me, I still fly with them and rarely have any problems.

Use Synergy Touchpoints to Handle Customer Complaints

Murphy's Law states that if anything can go wrong, it will. And when things go wrong, customers complain. The Synergy "WOW" Factor! approach gives you a proven approach for handling customer complaints, regardless of the problem's source.

"Right responses increase loyalty."

Synergy "WOW" Factor!

Follow Through
Stay Connected
Deliver
Under-Promise
Solution
Assure
Restate
Apologize
Take Notes
Listener
Customer Vent
Approachable
Proactive
Problem Solver

Here's what to do:

Be a **problem solver**.

Be **proactive** - stay calm.

Be **approachable** - attitude is vital.

Let the **customer vent**. Understand that they need to feel heard. Let them express their complaint.

Be an active **listener**. Pay attention and listen to your customer's main message.

Take notes and identify the main complaint area. You will need this to resolve the complaint.

Apologize - Once the customer has laid out their complaint, respond with a supportive statement. Always apologize first: **"I apologize."** Then say something such as: *"I heard you," "I apologize," "I understand,"* or *"Okay, I've got it."*

Restate their complaint with a confirmation question. "My understanding is that the problem is _____."

Assure the customer that you appreciate their business and will solve their problem.

Solution - Use a calm and supportive tone, show empathy, but be firm. Be very clear in communicating the exact and precise steps that will be taken for the solution. Follow up with an email.

Under-promise and over-deliver.

Deliver on the promise, and do it precisely as you promised.

Stay connected throughout the process.

Follow through and make sure the customer is satisfied with the end result.

Use Synergy Touchpoints to Turn Difficult Customers into Customers for Life!

The Synergy "WOW" Factor! approach is also extremely useful for dealing with difficult customers. The following chart will guide you in recognizing various personality types based on typical behaviors and then use synergy touchpoints to provide a "WOW" response.

Behaviors	"WOW" Response
Personality: Big Ego Bob . . . Me, Me, Me	
"Do you know who I am?" Impatient Name dropper Demands attention Rude and loud Aggressive	Stay calm and proactive. Remain professional. Apologize for the circumstances. Use a supportive tone: "Let me fix this for you." Act immediately—speed is vital.
Personality: Potty Mouth Patty	
Loud, crude, and drops "F-bombs" for effect Semi-narcissistic behavior: "The world revolves around me." Demanding	Stay calm and proactive. Maintain professional etiquette. Ignore insults, bad language, and accusations. Don't take it personally. Use open-ended questions. Loop back to solutions. "So, if we ___."

Chapter #5: Manage Your Customers' Expectations

Behaviors	"WOW" Response
Personality: Freaky Fred	
"You never know who you're going to get!" Nice one day, tantrum the next Huffs, puffs, sulks, complains Storms off Gunny sacks Online exaggeration	Be consistently calm – let him vent. Use support statements: "I understand." Always apologize. Use open-ended questions to determine the main problem and then fix it.
Personality: Controlling Candice	
Arrives with a list of what, how, and who should be doing things Will insist you do it her way Will badger you until you concede	Don't let this customer go to war with you. Nobody ever won an argument with a customer. Say "Yes" and do it quickly. When you can't "do the impossible," negotiate for what you *can* do. Always give feedback to the controller.

Synergy "WOW" Factor!

Behaviors	"WOW" Response
Personality: Cheap Charlie	
Wants everything for free; he's a freeloader "Get whatever you can." Use it, abuse it, bring it back; very manipulative As a tactic, accuses you of taking advantage	Be proactive. Be aware it's a game – see it as such. Be fair to all: you, your company, and the customer. Be candid but diplomatic, and always be gracious. Ask for details on manipulative claims. Stand firm. Negotiate as a last resort.
Personality: Indecisive Ivor	
Cannot decide; is insecure and wants to think about it Asks you what you think Is overly agreeable Will blame you if dissatisfied – you said ___.	Stay calm. Do not show frustration. Ask questions and lead. Do not decide for him. Double-check that the issue has been addressed.

Chapter #5: Manage Your Customers' Expectations

Behaviors	"WOW" Response
Personality: Viral Victor	
Low face-to-face response. Uses the Internet to voice opinions, anger, etc. Can be mean and make exaggerated comments about situations	Always respond. Check the validity of complaints. If valid, contact the customer and make it right. If valid, apologize immediately. If invalid, present your version with polite language.

Synergy "WOW" Factor!

Chapter Six:
Put Your Customers First

A customer is the most important person in any business. Unfortunately, many associates prioritize business goals and management demands above doing what's right for their customers. When you make meeting your sales goals for continued employment your first priority, this means your self-serving interests are coming first. Of course, achieving goals is important—I'm not disputing that. What I think is important is how these goals are achieved. If you emphasize your job's goals and don't broaden this to include your customer as the most important person in the business, then your boss' goals become much more important than serving your customers.

Always Act in the Customer's Interest

Acting in the customer's interest has much to do with who you believe is more important. If you work for a supervisor who believes she is the most important person in the business, you will act in her interest first because you want to keep your job. Conversely, if you work for a company that has a customer-driven culture and considers the customer as very important—and perhaps more important than any member of the executive team, including the CEO—you will act quite naturally in the customer's interest.

On a personal level, this has much to do with your mindset, what kind of energy you bring to work, and how much you enjoy serving and dealing with people. It just makes good business sense to act in the interest of the person who holds the key to current and long-term brand growth and revenue!

Know that when you put the Customer First, Magic Happens

I want to share with you a letter that I received a while back from a woman named Mary, who had participated in one of my programs. The story that Mary shared beautifully illustrates what can happen when the Synergy "WOW" Factor! principles are implemented.

Always remember: Without a customer, we would not have a business – Let's make them say: "WOW"!

Chapter #6: Put Your Customers First

Here is what the letter said…

Hi Chris,

Back in 2007, I bought my all-time favorite convertible, a MINI Cooper, at a local dealership. It had extremely low mileage, came with a service contract, and the salesperson was very professional, nice, not pushy, and left me alone to decide. I liked it, so a little later that day, I was cruising down Pacific Coast Highway with the top down. Life was good!

Unfortunately, sometime later, I totaled my MINI and was back in the market for another car. Checking back with the same salesperson at the local dealership where I had purchased the MINI (and doing additional research on the Internet), I discovered that the lowest mileage, the most reasonably-priced used car, was at the same dealership where I purchased the MINI.

This time, though, I wanted to opt for a car that didn't start every maintenance trip with "But it's a MINI," as the price went from $100 to $200 with every service visit. I loved the MINI, but it was expensive to service. Instead, I went with a Scion from the same dealership and the same salesperson, and I am very happy.

Several months later, my sister was ready to trade in her Nissan. I suggested she check out the dealership I had worked with and speak with the salesperson I had dealt with. She did and walked out with a brand new RAV4.

So, now this dealership had over $50,000 worth of no-cost-of-sale business that would not have happened had the service not been performed well.

The primary purpose of this letter is to validate your point that great service is a financial strategy as much as a service value.

Best wishes,
Mary

Today, more than ever, business has to be earned. Our customers have endless options on where and how to spend their money. When you put the customer first, magic happens. But without a "WOW" Factor! experience, they will take their business elsewhere. Don't give them a reason to do so.

Your customers are the sole reason that you are gainfully employed. Not your manager and not the CEO. Make it easy on yourself and do what you can to keep customers for life!

Wells Fargo did not put Customers First

While Mary's local car dealer obviously did things right, Wells Fargo did things completely wrong. Focusing on business goals instead of doing what's right for their customers led to one of the biggest banking scandals in recent U.S. history. Wells Fargo's example is a cautionary tale of what can happen when you take this wrong approach.

Here's what happened . . . in September 2016, Wells Fargo paid $185 million in fines for dishonest business practices. What did Wells Fargo do to deserve these fines? They created over two million unauthorized customer accounts! Investigators discovered that the pressure on employees to hit sales quotas was immense. There was daily and hourly measurement, personal pressure from supervisors to engage in unethical behavior, and a huge compensation system based heavily on bonuses. Earning these bonuses, of

Chapter #6: Put Your Customers First

course, required meeting unrealistically high sales quotas.

The fallout from this scandal for Wells Fargo's employees was enormous, and their professional reputations may never recover. Many were fired. At first, the blame for this unethical practice was placed on "a few rotten apples" in the sales team. Of course, it wasn't just the sales team. There was a system-wide lack of integrity and a toxic, self-serving culture.

Those who played ethically no doubt feel betrayed by the actions of upper management who arrogantly fought for repayment of incentives.

Digging deeper, more troubling practices were found. Many employees quit because of the immense pressure to engage in unethical sales practices, and many were fired for reporting these unethical practices through the company's hotline. And yes, senior leadership was aware of these aggressive sales practices going back to 2002.

There is a right way and a wrong way to make outstanding profits. Wells Fargo demonstrated the wrong way.

For the record, and in the interest of balance and fairness, Wells Fargo is now recognized as an excellent service bank.

Develop Synergy "WOW" Factor! Awareness

The "WOW" Factor! is your declaration of integrity. The right way to create outstanding profits is to make the customer the most important person in the business and then live up to that value. Throughout business history, this philosophy has always succeeded when implemented with integrity. When you develop Synergy "WOW" Factor! awareness, putting the customers' needs first, becomes easy.

Here are some tips for making this happen . . .

Tip #1: Be Approachable. A Customer is the Purpose of your Work, not an Interruption of it

Some people have approachable personalities. They welcome you, and you can sense that there is no reservation. They create very positive first impressions. On the other hand, other people are not approachable or service-oriented. They act as though a customer with a question interrupts more important work.

Needless to say, customers want to be welcomed, and they don't want to deal with interpersonal tension. Most people I know would prefer some appropriate levity and humor when dealing with service issues.

A true story about working retail during the holidays illustrates what happens when salespeople don't under-

Chapter #6: Put Your Customers First

stand that serving the customer is job number one—not an interruption of more important things.

Just after lunch, Henry, the Lead, spoke to Mary, one of the key associates.

"What happened right before lunch? Did someone ask for help and not get it?" Henry asked.

Mary explained that she had helped a customer who asked for a price check, which she provided. No problem. "What happened that you are asking, Henry?"

"I heard that a customer was looking to pick up an order she placed earlier," Henry replied. "Surprisingly, when she approached the clerk, the clerk was noticeably agitated by the request, responding that she only had an hour for lunch and did not have the time to pick up the item. Therefore, the customer should ask another clerk to help her. As it turned out, the item was already bagged and sitting on the shelf. It would have only taken about 10 seconds to satisfy the customer."

As Henry told the story, Mary became noticeably irritated. She complained that this clerk's poor attitude directly reflected on her and was not appreciated.

"It's not my fault," retorted Mary.

Mary's attitude took Henry by surprise. "Mary," he said, "it's not your fault, and neither is it mine, but it is your responsibility and the responsibility of anyone interfacing with the customer. We all need to own the idea that it's a privilege to serve them."

"Why should I own someone else's problem, Henry?" Mary asked.

"You are not owning their problem," Henry explained. "You own the idea that it's our responsibility as a team to own all customer issues and requests. That's the attitude and teamwork spirit that really gives us a competitive advantage."

Before leaving work for the day, Mary asked Henry if he'd discovered who had such unprofessional service. After that question, Henry realized that Mary had not shifted her mindset. He became acutely aware that asking people to serve the customer does not move them from being self-serving to serving others. They understand it but are not applying it, and that's where the rubber hits the road. Henry had a lot of work to get everyone to know that customers have many choices and it is an honor to serve them.

Tip #2: Make a Positive First Impression

"Your attitude speaks so loudly; I cannot hear what you are saying!"

Be aware of the impact of your behavior on others! Your approach is so important because first impressions count. While words are important, your body language often speaks louder than the words you speak. Be aware of both!

Good communication and a firm handshake speak volumes. People need eye contact and a sincere smile. Culturally, this is a sign of trust. Internationally, it's a sign of safe welcome. You will make a positive impression if you give your undivided, present-moment attention to the person you're trying to communicate with.

I recently took a much-needed vacation. After a long, exhausting trip, I found myself at the reception desk at my hotel. "Hi," I said. "My name is Chris Alexander. I have a reservation."

Without looking up, the person behind the counter said, "What's your name again?" One of the key elements in connecting with customers is making eye contact because that says, "I acknowledge you; I am the person who will take care of you."

"My name is Chris Alexander," I repeated.

"All right, just let me check. No, I don't see you listed here."

She still did not acknowledge me or make eye contact, and I could feel my blood beginning to boil. This was more than unprofessional—it was an "I couldn't care" attitude and a complete lack of awareness. Was she ever trained to make the customer feel comfortable?

"I know you have my reservation," I stated, "because I have the confirmation letter."

"Spell your name for me," she said, still not making eye contact.

"A L E X....."

"Oh, wait!" she exclaimed, "Yes, here it is. I was looking under Oleander."

Did this make me say "WOW"? No! All it did was raise my stress level. "WOW"! What a bad first impression!

From that moment on, I felt apprehensive about the hotel. To top this bad service, there wasn't one word of apology for her behavior. The real kicker from her was when she made brief eye contact and asked, with a slight blink and tiny smile, "Sir, you will notice a customer service questionnaire in your packet; if you don't mind, would you complete it for me?"

My reaction: Sure, but you won't like what I tell management about the service you provided!

Tip #3: Be Courteous

"It is so much easier to be nice—to be respectful, to put yourself in your customers' shoes, and try to understand how you might help them before they ask for help than trying to mend a broken customer relationship."
                                                                -Mark Cuban

Customer service is about being courteous and having good manners, which is now considered a work-related skill. Because manners are no longer practiced as a civil social value, you must practice manners at work to "WOW" your customers. Customers are always "WOW"ed by being appreciated, respected, and valued.

If you, like many in today's society, were not taught civility and good manners when you were growing up, now is the time to learn respectful communication! As the saying goes, you can catch many more bees with honey than vinegar. In other words, it's much easier to get what you want—in this case, a happy customer—by being courteous and polite than by being rude.

When I was growing up, we were all taught the magic words: *"please," "thank you"* (not just "thanks"), and *"you're welcome."* These weren't optional—they were a basic part of showing respect. In today's business environment, things may be more casual—both in dress and in demeanor—but courtesy should never go out of style. Customers still want to feel valued, and sometimes it's the simplest gestures that make the biggest difference. Using these magic words—*"please," "thank you,"* and *"you're welcome"*—is a small effort with a big impact.

Tip #4: Be the First-Giver

Your customers want to know: *"Are you ready to solve my problems?" "Do you have the tools to take care of me?" "Do you intend to take care of me? Will you deliver on your promise, or do I have to jump through hoops while you play by some handbook or scripted response?"*

You can be a first-giver by being willing to serve first, with a *"how-can-I-help-you?"* demeanor. A willing, helpful attitude is an international language, and most people will respond very positively. Being the first-giver is grounded in the law of reciprocity. Mostly, if you treat them positively, they will respond positively to you. The law of reciprocity supports the principle that if you "WOW" a customer, that customer will "WOW" you with referrals and repeat business.

Being a first-giver is about knowing that a win/win mentality is focused on growth. What goes around, comes around. Being a first-giver requires a shift in thinking to *"It's-all-about-you"* and *"You are the most important person to me right at this moment."*

Chapter #6: Put Your Customers First

Hi Chris!

We were in Hawaii at a conference where you were the keynote speaker on building customer loyalty through teamwork and service from the inside out. You talked about the importance of having a first-giver service attitude and how that can repay you from places you least expect it. You called it the "law of reciprocity."

Your words were not even cold when I experienced precisely what you wanted us to grasp. Right after lunch, a few of us went looking for Hawaiian shirts. I had a hard time finding something I liked. On the other hand, several people in the group quickly found shirts they liked. I was frustrated and just about to move on when I heard the owner say, "Excuse me, sir, but you are a winner today! Every day, I give away one of the discounted shirts. It starts my day off right, and I hope it will do the same for you! Go ahead. Pick one."

Surprisingly, I found a very cool black ukulele shirt. I, of course, thanked him and asked if this was a good business idea. "It's the aloha spirit, sir! We appreciate our customers." I was on my way out, but not before finding and purchasing another two shirts I liked.

While walking back to the conference, your words, "giving a little mostly results in reciprocity", came to mind. That shop owner somehow knew that to give first was the key.

The attitude the shop owner demonstrated toward customer service was very impressive. Every time I wear that black Hawaiian shirt; I think about that experience. I tell anyone going to Maui about it, too! I have become his very inexpensive salesperson! I will never buy a Hawaiian shirt anywhere else. Why would I? He has a customer for life.

Best regards,
George

"WOW" Affirmation

I "WOW" customers by listening to them and being responsive to their suggestions, which helps me to serve them better.

I am not offended by their questions. I am not defensive, argumentative, or sarcastic, even when I think I am right.

It's my job to create a trusting relationship that leads to loyalty. "WOW"ing my customer means I have listened to their voice, and I understand that it's up to me to manage and exceed their expectations.

A Story of Principled Reciprocal Service

Two boys were playing a game of hide and seek in the Scottish Highlands marshlands. One was a poor farmer's son, and the other was the son of a wealthy vacationing lord from England. While hiding some distance away, the farmer's son heard a desperate cry for help. Running toward the sound, he came upon a deep bog in which the other boy was stuck up to his chest, screaming and sinking deeper. Panicked and not knowing what to do, the farmer's son looked around for something to use to pull the boy out of the bog.

Nearby, he found a broken tree branch and quickly returned to the bog. He stretched out over the bog with the branch in hand, shouting to the boy to reach for it. Keeping one hand on the branch, he secured himself with his other hand on a rock, giving him solid pulling leverage. After a mighty struggle, pulling with all his strength, it seemed for a moment that the boy would surely perish. Exhausted but determined and with one last mighty pull, the bog loosened, and released the boy covered in mud and peat. Both boys lay there for a while and then ran to their respective homes.

The next day, the lord's carriage arrived at the farmer's humble abode. An aristocratic, well-dressed man stepped out of the carriage and introduced himself as the father of the saved boy. "Was it you who saved my son's life yesterday?" he asked the farmer.

"It wasn't me," said the farmer. "It was my son, Sire."

"Here . . . I have a reward for him. I must repay him for what he did."

"I don't want payment," the farmer replied. "I have taught my son to have good values, and anyone with good values would have done the same."

At that moment, the farmer's son appeared at the farmhouse door. "Is that your son?" the lord asked.

"Yes," said the farmer proudly.

"I have an idea. Let me pay for his education. If he's like his father, he'll grow into a man we'll both be proud of."

Based on that idea and wanting the best for his son, the farmer accepted the gift.

Many years later, the lord was once more faced with the tragedy of potentially losing his son. This time not to the bog but to what was in those days a deadly disease, pneumonia. His attending doctors said there was no hope, that his son would only live for a few more days, maybe a week at most. The lord began to pray. He begged that his son be spared and that he would overcome his illness.

As if it were divine intervention, the lord's butler blurted out that he had heard of a young researcher working on a powerful new medicine that might cure the lord's son.

Chapter #6: Put Your Customers First

"Go with great haste and bring the young researcher here immediately!" ordered the lord.

The researcher arrived several hours later. From his bag, he brought out what we now know as a hypodermic syringe that he proceeded to fill with a cream-colored liquid, which he injected into the sickly young man's buttocks.

The next morning, as if a miracle had taken place, the lord's son woke up asking for food! He was on his way to recovery!

Who were these people in the story?

The boy who fell in the bog and later came down with pneumonia was Sir Winston Churchill, the Prime Minister of England and historic leader of the Allied forces in World War II. Had his life not been saved, history would have been very different.

Who was the farmer's son? . . . Sir Alexander Fleming. With the help of Lord Randolph Churchill, he attended the very best schools, graduated from St. Mary's Medical School, London University, and later became the world-renowned Nobel prize-winning scientist and discoverer of penicillin. Penicillin, the very same substance he injected into Winston, to save his life.

What does this legend or story have to do with the Synergy "WOW" Factor!?

It's a story of two men who lived by strong human service principles and, through those principles, tapped into several profound life-changing laws that, in their case, altered the course of humanity. The first is the law of reciprocity. When Winston was saved from the bog, Lord Randolph reciprocated by paying for Alexander's education. Years later, Alexander reciprocated by saving Sir Winston's life again. Both young men then changed the course of world events through a selfless commitment to service.

What would have happened if Alexander had not started the process? That's how service begins—by somebody giving first. That's why we say taking ownership of the Synergy "WOW" Factor! is your declaration of integrity.

You simply say, "I believe in the principle of service in a way that will astound you. I understand that without you, we would have no business. So, just as Lord Randolph would have lost his son if Alexander didn't save him, I will plant the seed first by giving great service and thus begin the process of reciprocity."

Tip #5: Do not Attempt to Argue or Battle Wits with a Customer

Even worse than simply being discourteous is to take things a step further and attempt to argue with a customer.

No one has ever won an argument with a customer. You can win the argument, but in doing so, you may lose the customer.

Social media loves to spread tales of poor service more so than stories of a positive nature. Why risk your business' reputation by refusing a reasonable request or getting into an unwinnable battle? Of course, in some instances, the request may not be so reasonable. So what?

> *"You can always find a way to please a customer"*

Never underestimate the cost of losing a customer.

Fun fact: Nordstrom, as you may know, does not sell snow tires. However, they have taken them as a return.

Tip #6: Check your Ego at the Door

When Quincy Jones re-recorded "We are the World" for the refugees in Haiti, he posted a huge sign outside the studio that read, "Leave your ego at the door." That sign affected all the big personalities who participated in the recording and synergized the performance. The song became extremely popular and came off with so much positive energy that it was felt worldwide!

On the other hand, when your ego is in the way you are likely to say stupid stuff, become unbearable, and think you are invincible! Mike Jeffries, then CEO of Abercrombie & Fitch, made one of the biggest ego statements that can only make you ask, "What was he thinking?"

"We go after the cool kids," he said. "We go after the attractive, all-American kid with a great attitude and many friends. Many people don't belong [in our clothes] and can't belong. Are we exclusionary? Absolutely. That's why we hire good-looking people in our stores, because good-looking people attract other good-looking people, and we want to market to cool, good-looking people. We don't market to anyone other than that."

Needless to say, Jeffries' comments created a tornado of negativity throughout traditional and social media. Why? Because he was talking about excluding certain groups based on body shaming. He said that if you or your kid are wearing a size large, you aren't cool enough to wear our logo. Based on all of its messaging and advertising, Abercrombie & Fitch's corporate leaders also seemed to embrace the "thin-only" image.

Parents were disgusted and organized a grassroots movement that really damaged Jeffries and the company. Mike Jeffries was forced to resign. Instead of taking responsibility, he suggested that his comments were taken out of context.

One would think that the negative, very costly experience faced by Abercrombie & Fitch would be a lesson learned by every smart company in that space and maybe beyond. Yet, some individuals still fail to realize the impact such statements can have. Don't they understand that if a statement is spoken on social media, it's recorded and replayed?

Unfortunately, many speak first and then follow up with damage control.

How about this one? "Frankly, some women's bodies just don't work [for the $100 yoga pants]," Chip Wilson, CEO of Lululemon, said on Bloomberg TV's "Street Smart" program. "It's really more about the rubbing through the thighs, how much pressure is there over a while, and how much they use it."

Instead of listening to their customers regarding the product and then using that valuable information to improve products and customer satisfaction dramatically, Wilson blamed the issue on the customer's body, specifically, the customer's "not thin" body.

It was amazing that these two highly intelligent people, who were at the top of their game, could fall so hard.

As the stories of these two men illustrate, an unbalanced ego can be very dangerous! I'm using the term "unbalanced" to understand that we all have self-protective egos, and a balanced ego is an important part of self-preservation. It gives us drive, determination, and real confidence.

An unbalanced ego, on the other hand, stems from insecurity, which often plays out in the following ways:

- a superiority complex
- fear of loss
- mistrust
- social withdrawal
- jealousy
- silos
- victim mentality

A major problem with self-serving customer service reps is that they don't listen. Yet, the most flattering thing you can do in any relationship is listen to what a person says. Everyone wants to be heard. CSRs who don't check their egos at the door also don't think about how their words and actions may impact others.

An unbalanced ego limits your ability to listen to others and consider other people's concerns.

A customer comes to us for goods or services or to have problems solved. It is our job to provide solutions that make them say, "WOW!"

Tip #7: Be Present. Giving Undivided Attention shows you Care

"First you, then me. Be present with customers!"

The most flattering compliment you can give your customers is to be present with them. Being present enables you to:

- sense your customer's mood and energy
- show your customer you care
- make your customer the most important person in the business
- build relationship trust
- elevate brand perception.

Plus, being present gives you a chance to practice your listening skills. Eventually, you'll develop the ability to "hear between the lines" and glean information that will enable you to serve your customers' needs better.

Each interaction you have with a customer influences their buying experience. Each interaction is another touchpoint. Suppose you are in the present and empathic to your customer's problem; this creates a touchpoint that forms a synergy, elevating the customer's perception of the level of service you provide.

Being more conscious and in the present moment is a liberating experience, but doing so takes practice. Being in the present moment involves becoming more aware of yourself—which can be scary, especially if you are afraid to change or cannot accept that you need to change. An awareness of why you love what you do is extremely powerful, motivational, and inspirational. However, greater personal and situational awareness is the path to greater personal growth and joy in the workplace. Knowing who you are is always a path to understanding the actions and behaviors of others, which helps considerably in remaining proactive with internal and external customers.

The practice of being in the present moment is the essence of outstanding customer communication. Your customer will notice if your thoughts wander away from the service conversation. You will also miss hearing vital information, which can result in a low-rated customer survey. Or, worse, you may lose that customer to the competition.

> *"Life is too short not to be in the present!"*

It is easy to let your thoughts wander. However, if you stay in the present and give your customers your undivided attention, they will be "WOW"ed by your immediate and effective responsiveness. It's flattering, works extremely well, and benefits any business transaction.

Chapter #6: Put Your Customers First

I know I have had weird experiences dealing with customer service representatives who were not present. For example, I recently had to talk with my mobile phone company about my endless problems with my phone.

The person who answered the phone seemed professional enough, although somewhat scripted. Too bad my mobile phone company didn't know that phony voices and computerized scripting do not enhance the "WOW" Factor! In fact, they may reduce the value of the brand. Here's how the conversation went . . .

CSR: "How can I help you today?"

Me: "Well, I'm hoping you can. This is the third replacement of my phone, which still has a sharp sound for incoming calls and an echo for the person I'm calling. I want it replaced."

CSR: "Okay, have you tried to reprogram your phone?"

Me: "No, I haven't done that, and that's not what I want to do. Right now, I want to solve my problem."

CSR: "Let's go through all the steps, shall we? That should fix your phone."

Me: "I don't want you to ask me what I've done in the past because you should have the awareness to know that if I'm on my third phone, I've been there and done that!"

CSR: "Okay, let me ask you some questions, so I'll be able to help you."

Synergy "WOW" Factor!

Me: "Okay, are these new questions? I went through many questions already with someone else—three times now."

CSR: "Do you know who you talked to?"

Me: "No, I don't remember, but I need you to know that I want to replace this phone, not jump through more hoops."

CSR: "Okay, when you talked to the last person, you should've got his name and, in this way..."

Me: "Excuse me, I apologize for interrupting you, but we have already been on the phone for five minutes, and I waited for twenty-five minutes to reach you! I just need your authorization code or someone to replace my phone."

CSR: "We did that until last month but changed our policy. It's a pity you didn't call a month ago; I could've authorized it then."

At this point, it became obvious that I was getting angry.

CSR: "Hold on, sir, I'm putting you through to my supervisor."

Me: "Okay, maybe he or she will help."

Five-minute delay.

Supervisor: "Good morning!"

Me: "Morning."

Chapter #6: Put Your Customers First

Supervisor: "Sir, I believe you are having a problem with your phone."

Me: "Yes!"

Supervisor: "What can I do for you today?"

Hooray! A person who is in a state of NOW!

Me: "I have had two previous phones. I want a new one that works or a reimbursement."

Supervisor: "I want you to have that, too. Let me make that happen for you."

Me: Hooray! Someone from the world of "WOW"!

Supervisor: "Sir, I have all your details in front of me. You certainly have had a lot of problems. I apologize! I have your mailing address and will send you the upgraded model today. When you receive it, the instructions will be in the box; just send the old phone back to us. Test your new phone and call me if you need any help getting it perfect. My name is Mandy, and my direct number is 1-800-xxx-xxxx."

"WOW"! Same company, same customer, same problem. One person was fully present, considered what was happening, and immediately solved my problem. The other person was not present enough to think about my situation and what it would take actually to solve my problem; instead, they stuck with a script that, from my perspective, made things worse.

Tip #8: Use Active Listening Loopback Process

The greatest way to show respect for another person is to listen. The best way to negotiate, set goals, and make sales is to listen to your customers. The best way to get along with your coworkers is to take the time to hear what they're saying to you. When you listen, shut out your mental voice and concentrate fully on what the other person is saying. Put aside your comments, doubts, and questions. If those things are important, they'll come back to you later!

Listen with your whole self. Since 85% of communication comes in a non-verbal way, it's easier to really know what someone is saying when you're sitting face-to-face. However, you can also follow clues on the phone, such as pauses, repetitions, and hesitations.

Use your intuition and empathy to tune into what the other person may feel while you talk.

Be aware that it's more likely that a business relationship will end due to poor interpersonal relationships rather than money. Not everyone is seeking the same thing, and it is essential to understand their dominant buying motive. You need to listen between the lines. Watch for body language and voice tone and see if you feel the energy.

If you're not sure you understand what is being said, it's a good practice to loopback what you think is the gist of what they're trying to communicate. This way, they can correct you if you're wrong, clarify a point, or agree with you if you're right. This is a "Listening Loopback Process." Some of the biggest messes can be avoided by checking to determine that you correctly understand what the other person is saying.

The Listening Loopback Process means that you listen and then loop it back to the customer with a clarifying question. This process requires listening carefully, paraphrasing what is heard, and restating it to ensure the problem, request, or situation is understood and agreed upon. When doing this, always start with a support statement, such as "*I understand.*" You want to put the customer at ease by showing them that you are present.

The Listening Loopback Process helps you:

- identify the dominant complaint, problem, or issue
- simplify the discussion and stay on track
- identify the solution
- identify the customer's justifying statements
- identify positive and negative statements
- begin with a supporting statement, like: *"I understand"*

Listening Loopback Process example:

Customer: "Things are just too expensive these days. Not long ago, you could still pay cash for all your products. Today, it's impossible. I need the best prices because I need products for my business. I'm talking about $1,000 or more per order. Nothing is cheap anymore."

What is the customer's dominant message? "I need products for my business." This is the issue that needs to be solved. This is the customer's buying motive.

What is the customer's main objection? "Things are just too expensive these days."

What is the customer's justifying statement? "I'm talking about $1,000 or more."

What are the customer's negative statements? The negative statements are: "Today it's impossible" and "Nothing is cheap anymore."

Here is a feedback statement that could be used to respond to this customer. Read it carefully, learn how to respond, build bridges and create the "WOW" Factor!

"I understand. So, you are saying that you need a financial package that will keep your orders under $1,000 each. Am I right?"

 Write out several common complaints you encounter daily with customers and practice this process.

Tip #9: Be Proactive and Empathetic

Being proactive means taking action before something happens rather than just responding to things after the fact. Being empathetic means experiencing an awareness of how others (such as your customers!) feel. Empathetic proactiveness involves responding positively to situations with emotional intelligence.

When you are proactive and empathetic you can better connect with your customers and even overcome the negativity that is associated with dissatisfied customers. This is because an authentic concern will often calm an irate customer.

Empathetic proactiveness begins with a good relationship with yourself. When you feel good about yourself, you feel good about others. When you trust yourself, you can trust others. Accepting yourself, "warts and all," you can also accept others unconditionally. When you set others free from your judgments and comparisons, you allow your customers the freedom to be themselves. This might mean that they may be obnoxious, arrogant, difficult, and downright rude from time to time—and that's just being human! Your job is to calm them down, maintain objectivity, and not take it personally.

Today's customers are seeking more than just a good price. They seek recognition, added value, and a sense that you're there for them. Admittedly somewhat melodramatic, customers now demand more from products and services. Plus, they want a great experience. When you are proactive and empathetic, this influences their perception, and their perception influences their experience.

Some customers will abuse you. They will be mean and angry before they call you. Their anger may not even have anything to do with your company. Because they lack emotional intelligence, they want to unload all that negativity on someone. You do not have to tolerate violent, aggressive people. They are not looking to be "WOW"ed but for someone to beat up.

When these situations arise, avoid personal confrontation. Remain calm and do your best to help them get what they want. Mostly, they are looking for a freebie. It makes them feel as though they've won! If you have tried everything within your power to be empathetic and they are still frothing at the mouth, redirect them to your manager.

Your manager will support you! Some customers are extremely expensive to maintain. Send them to your competitor.

I'd like to share how one employee's proactiveness helped defuse a customer's anger.

I was flying up to San Francisco. I boarded the plane, sat, and began making myself comfortable, hoping no one would sit beside me.

As I relaxed, the pilot came over the intercom, saying our flight would be delayed for a few minutes due

Chapter #6: Put Your Customers First

to a passenger checking in from an international connection. I heard some people grumbling, but I didn't mind. It was only an hour's flight up to San Francisco, and the pilot could easily make up the time in the air.

Just then, a huge mountain of a man appeared in the walkway of the plane. He was about 6 feet 8 inches tall and at least three feet wide. My first impression was that he was a bodybuilder, wrestler, or, maybe in a previous life, an Olympic weightlifter. He was sweating, breathing heavily, carrying his bags, and heading directly toward me.

In a booming voice, he said, "You are in my seat."

He was right. I had inadvertently sat in his seat. I quickly scooted over, and he sat down with a huge thud. The whole plane shook.

He immediately started complaining about everything: the seats, the airport, the flight attendant! "She just has this job because she's trying to catch a husband," he scoffed.

Would I have to listen to this man for the next hour? Maybe I'll shift seats once the seat belt lights are off.

Soon, the flight attendant brought snacks and he started complaining to her about the packet size.

"You call this a snack? This isn't a snack! This is an insult!" he complained.

"What's wrong with it, sir?" the flight attendant asked.

"You want me to tell you what's wrong with it?" he responded.

"Yes, please, sir," she said.

"Well, it's a bad snack. A very bad snack!" he said.

The flight attendant took the snack from him, paused, looked around, and then, pointing her finger at the snack packet, said, "Bad snack, bad snack!"

Of course, everyone laughed, including my seatmate!

I was so impressed by the flight attendant's proactiveness that, as we were leaving the plane, I stopped and asked her how she had responded so quickly.

She smiled and answered, "Oh, I wasn't so quick. I was prepared. Last week, it was "bad pretzel, bad pretzel." I always have a few lines ready for situations like that. Otherwise, I would be quite frustrated and react negatively, and I need this job. Our passengers are tired and stressed, and I must do my part to care for their needs."

I realized she had been taught the principles of world-class service. She demonstrated a perfect proactive and empathetic attitude.

Here's a story that demonstrates empathy…even when faced with a belligerent customer.

Everyone loves a great deal, and there isn't one better than the Costco lunch hot dog and drink for around

Chapter #6: Put Your Customers First

$1.50 plus tax or a big slice of pizza for something like 1.99. The lines, although long, are generally calm, and people are respectful of one another. But not on this day.

I was waiting to buy my lunch when suddenly, pushing her way through the crowd to the front of the line, an obnoxious and blatantly rude woman yelled at Brian, the server, "Give me a f**ing cup, you moron!" Instantaneously, there was silence. Even the clink-clink of the ice machines stopped. Hot dogs sat gaping, waiting to be dressed. Business conversations were put on hold. Moms and their kids were about to gain a story to tell Dad. This woman had everyone's attention. The entire crowd shifted their focus to the confrontation brewing at poor Brian's window.

To his credit, Brian stayed calm and empathetic. Brian had no issue with giving her a cup if she simply told him why she needed an additional cup.

Her response was, "I don't have a cup! Are you hard of hearing? Give me a f**ing cup now!"

Suddenly, a steely little old lady stepped forward from the back of the line. She sternly said, "He's trying to help you. Be nice. It may even change your life."

Whoa, was this the moment where the heroine swoops in to save the young man from the wrath of the wicked witch? Now face-to-face, Kate (the little old lady with nerves of steel and fists balled up) stepped forward and said, in an unwavering

Synergy "WOW" Factor!

and firm voice like a commander in chief, "Apologize to Brian, right now!"

Well, what do you know? The obnoxious woman stepped back and apologized. Then, she broke down in tears right when security arrived. Isn't that the way it goes with bullies?

Then someone in the crowd yelled, "NO SODA FOR YOU!" This displeased Brian. Being the empathetic person he is, Brian gave the security guard a cup to give to the obnoxious woman to fill up before being escorted off the property, all to the loud applause of the crowd! Sadly, this woman's behavior resulted in her being banned from all Costco locations. Some customers are not worth having.

Why did Kate confront this customer? "Because this was Brian!" she exclaimed. "He's the friendliest server you would ever want to meet. He remembers your name. He knows what you order every day. He is like a grandson! So polite!" Kate saw no option but to defend Brian after he received such harsh treatment.

Tip #10: Pay Attention to Diversity

Of course, every individual is unique and requires an approach suitable to their background. Cultural diversity is also an important part of workplace communication. People from different cultures have different ways of behaving, expectations, and outlooks on life. When working with people from different cultures, it's important to pay attention to these things to prevent or repair misunderstandings. Especially in today's global climate, it makes good sense to become educated about the mores and norms in the cultures of the people you work with.

Another aspect of diversity is that people from different generations often have different ways of looking at things. Realizing millennials are different than baby boomers—and require a different communication style—is key to a "WOW" Factor! level of customer service.

There are often differences between men and women, and people from different regions of the country. The more you can successfully increase your awareness and ability to connect and communicate with people who are different, the more successful you will be.

Tip #11: Treat Internal Customers as Well as you Treat External Customers

In your job, you have both internal customers and external customers. Internal customers are people or organizations that help your company to achieve its goals. This includes teammates, suppliers, consultants, etc. External customers are the people who purchase your products and services.

If you want to shine and provide "WOW" Factor! experiences, you must learn to shine with your internal customers first. Treat them with the same respect you would show an external customer. Within your organization, the "WOW" Factor! works from the inside out. Be aware that internal and external customers are integral to your success.

> *"When we treat each other with dignity, respect, and efficiency, we create a high-performance culture that ripples out to the customer"*

A while back, a CSR selected a few items and went to the only open cashier to pay for them. The cashier was on the phone talking to someone about a personal issue. The CSR waited for acknowledgment, such as, "I'll be with you shortly" or "Thank you for waiting." Instead, the cashier was focused on her conversation. She did not acknowledge the waiting CSR at all.

Chapter #6: Put Your Customers First

The CSR knew this was not the typical response a "customer" would receive. It appeared that the cashier did not think an internal customer had the same value as an external customer! Evidently, resolving her issue was much more important to her than serving a customer.

After her five-minute conversation ended, the cashier asked the CSR, "Are you working today?" That did not give the CSR a warm feeling because, yes, she was working today, and now she needed to rush upstairs to be on time.

This kind of simple interpersonal interaction causes internal negativity and a lack of respect. We should never underestimate how, if we treat an internal customer poorly, this can create behaviors that become a communication norm.

> *"The "WOW" Factor! is all about your attitude and how you make the customer experience magical and memorable!"*

Synergy "WOW" Factor!

Chapter Seven:
Be a Problem Solver

"Learn to like solving problems; success follows a problem solved!"

Regarding your product or service, you are more experienced and knowledgeable than your customer, which means you are in an excellent position to be a problem solver. Whether you are a salesperson or a CSR, your job is to solve your customer's problems. Find solutions and help them!

Maybe you have heard the same complaint a thousand times before. Some customers don't read the instructions. Some are downright rude. No, your customers are not always right, but so what? You still want their business!

"WOW"ing a customer requires problem-solving skills and the desire to go the extra mile for resolution. Why should the customer stay if you don't have a proper service attitude? No doubt someone else will work smarter and harder to attract their business.

Eight problem solving steps:

Step #1: Introduce Yourself Clearly

Start by introducing yourself clearly and ensuring the customer knows your name and title. Then, be sure you pronounce the customer's name correctly. Nothing can be more irritating—and even insulting to a frustrated customer than dealing with someone who has not paid attention to learn who they are speaking with.

Step #2: Ask Questions

Rudyard Kipling's poem, "Six Honest Serving Men," is a perfect tool to help solve problems and "WOW" customers:

> *There are six honest serving men, they show me what to do. Their names are: What? Where? When? How? Why? and Who?*

These open-ended problem-solving question starters keep the customer engaged and demonstrate your interest in solving their problem. Using these questions shows your customer that you want to learn how to meet their needs.

Chapter #7: Be a Problem Solver

Using the "six honest serving men" to determine the customer's dominant issue sends a message of your interest and concern and keeps everyone in the present moment. It is a great tool for problem-solving and can be applied as a root cause analysis or planning tool.

For example, you can ask:

- What can I help you with today?
- When did you purchase this product?
- Why [i.e., for what use] did you purchase this product?
- What exactly happened?
- When did it go wrong?
- Who else uses this product besides yourself?
- Where was the product kept?
- How can I help your situation?
- Where would you like me to ship your replacement?

Step #3: Listen Carefully

When you ask questions, listen carefully and attentively when the customer speaks. Gather all the facts. Be patient and deliberate, and do not rush. Once you've written things down, use the Listening Loopback Process to feed it to the customer to show you clearly understand the problem. This will ensure that you hear exactly what their concerns are. After feeding the information back, ask for a confirmation on exactly what the problem is.

Step #4: Thank and Apologize

Always thank your customers for raising complaints. After all, they have done you a favor by allowing you to fix the situation. Apologize for any inconvenience. Show them that you understand how they feel by your voice tone, body language, and attitude.

Step #5: Own the Problem

Show genuine concern and interest in their problem, even if you did not cause it. As a team member, you own a problem if it is addressed to you. You also own the responsibility for the solution.

Never say, "It's not my job" or "Hey, I only work here." Go the extra mile by spending the time necessary to develop an equitable solution for all. Instead, say, "What can I do to make it right?" The "WOW" Factor! depends on taking personal responsibility to be engaged and improve your knowledge constantly.

A customer is not a cold statistic. Customers are human beings with emotions and prejudices and need to be understood. They care about getting their problems solved and receiving fair value for their money. On behalf of the company, you own the problem and need to do whatever you can to resolve it.

Step #6: State your Company's Position

Once you have all the information and details, state your company's position regarding the situation or problem. You must avoid being defensive or rigid. Always remember that customers don't have to do business with you. When your customer has a problem, you must solve it to ensure their loyalty.

Customers are picky, and they don't have to understand. It's your job to understand and hold on to the customer.

Step #7: Be Honest and Sincere

When you or the company has made a mistake, admit it. When you don't admit your mistakes, you introduce doubt and uncertainty into the customer's level of trust in you and your brand. Transparency builds trust and neutralizes defensive egos. Being honest and sincere will allow you to move on and solve the problem and not be stuck on who's right or wrong. Normally, customers don't start off being mad. That comes about when they are lied to or hear endless excuses.

Step #8: State How You will Fix the Situation

Tell customers how you will resolve the situation. Come to an agreement with them on a solution. Then, fix the problem and follow up. Let them know each step of the way how close things are or when the problem will be solved. Be responsible and reliable. When you say you will do something within a given period, the customer expects you to live up to and deliver on your promise. Actions speak louder than words. Demonstrate your trustworthiness by living up to your word.

Always try to solve the problem quickly to regain their loyalty and trust. It is common knowledge that customers reaffirm their loyalty to companies that solve their problems quickly.

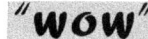

Step #8: State how you will fix the situation
Step #7: Be honest and sincere
Step #6: State your company's position
Step #5: Own the problem
Step #4: Thank and apologize
Step #3: Listen carefully
Step #2: Ask questions
Step #1: Introduce yourself clearly

Chapter #7: Be a Problem Solver

A Problem-Solving Success Story

The letter had to be marked before 6:00 p.m., and it was 5:55 p.m.! "OMG, only five minutes left. I need to make it. Otherwise, I lose $500,000!" thought Rich. Rushing toward the FedEx clerk, Rich was met with, "We've already sent and received our last packages of the day. We're closed."

Undeterred and looking directly into her eyes, Rich said quietly, "If this doesn't go out tonight, I will lose $500,000." He explained it was an insurance claim and the letter needed to go that night.

"Okay, sir. Let's see what we can do for you," the clerk replied. "Of course, you must share your $500,000 with the team here at FedEx." Smiling at her joke and relieved, Rich handed over the letter. It was as if time stood still; everything slowed down, and the sound of the ticking clock was deafening. Oh no! Turns out the address listed was a post office box, and only the U.S. Postal Service can deliver to a post office box.

"What can I do?" the clerk asked. "Can you email?"

"No," Rich said. "It must be a physical copy. Wait, here's an old-fashioned fax number! Can you believe they are still in use? That would work!"

Finally: "Transmission successful." Just in the nick of time!

You must admire how the FedEx agent handled the problem for Rich. Instead of refusing to help, she stepped up, gave selfless service, and exceeded what could be expected of her. She proactively put on her problem-solving hat and went to work. When Rich asked how she remained so calm under pressure, she answered with an insightful and wry little grin, "I'm a mom. I have three kids, so I know how to deal with last-minute pressure."

The clerk did an excellent job. Her focus immediately switched from "Gotta go" to "I have to help." She has the "WOW" Factor! gene. Once she understood the seriousness of the problem, she did whatever was required.

It is important to remember that most CSRs actually like people and want to help. Helping others boosts their self-esteem. The agent undoubtedly gave herself an atta gal! for resolving the problem.

Chapter #7: Be a Problem Solver

Chapter Eight: Examine your Perceptions about Work

> *"There is joy in work. There is no happiness except realizing that we have accomplished something."*
> -Henry Ford

What does it mean to you when you talk about the world of work? Does it make you smile, or do you cringe inside? Is work a painful necessity and the thing you do between weekends, or is it the thing you do because it brings you joy?

For most people, work is not a happy part of life. You're not imagining things: The world of work can be an unhappy and even emotionally dangerous place, but it doesn't have to be that way.

Whether you realize it or not, perception colors everything in your life, including your thoughts about work.

Your perceptions, of course, will impact your attitudes and your interactions with your customers. It's hard to provide Synergy "WOW" Factor! service if your perception is that your job is horrible, your customers and co-workers are all jerks and idiots, etc. This is why it's so important that you examine your perceptions about work.

Think Back to your Childhood

Chances are your perceptions about work started in your childhood. When your parents came home from work, how did they act? Did Mom collapse onto the sofa, complaining that she had a "hard day" at work and needed to rest? Did Dad take off his shoes, turn on the TV, and grouch at you not to bother him because he needed to "relax"? Did they act like someone who had an invigorating, exciting, enjoyable day at work—or someone who had experienced the opposite? Maybe you saw your parents' negative behaviors when you were little and thought, "Oh boy, work surely must be some awful place. Hope I never have to go there!"

Contrast this with Mr. Rogers, the children's public television star. He would come through the door, hang his suit jacket neatly in the closet, pull out a powder-blue cardigan, remove his shiny shoes, and put on his play shoes. Then he would take us into wonderland. Mr. Rogers was coming to work in a gentle, loving, imaginative place where people were friends, disagreements were solved, and he was happy.

What if everyone's work felt like Mr. Rogers' Neighborhood instead of a battle zone? It can! Why shouldn't you believe that assertion? You don't have to; just keep an open mind.

Remember tracing the alphabet on that big-lined paper with a fat pencil? Or drawing pictures with every color you could find? Or dancing freely to music, just because it felt good? Back then, trying hard—and succeeding—was fun!

Work may have changed, but your possibilities haven't. The key is perspective. Allowing for the possibility that work can be joyful is the first step toward making it a happy place.

Don't let Inaccurate Perceptions Wreck your Reality

Let's say you're going to a party, and right before you get there, someone tells you that the hostess said something particularly nasty about you last week. But you have to go to the party because you're supposed to network with someone you have few other chances of seeing. So you go, but you're miserable the whole time. Your hostess greets you at the door with a warm hug, and you think, "You hypocrite, get your hands off me," but you don't say anything. You're angry—

what did you ever do to her? Boy, would you like to tell her off! Or, feeling hurt, you wish you could ask her what you did to make her hate you so much.

Your unhappiness colors the whole party. But once you got home, you check your messages and discover it was a complete misunderstanding. Your informant feels terrible—he had heard wrong. Suddenly, you see the party in a different light. Your perceptions have changed.

Here's another story about the potentially devastating impact when there's a disconnect between perception and reality. This disconnect happened to Ron, a successful Southern California business owner . . . and the result was not pretty.

Ron, a car enthusiast who owns several late-model sports cars, is also the proud owner of a "getaway" mountain cottage in Big Bear, California. He and his wife often drive up to Big Bear to spend the weekend in a more relaxed environment.

On one of these occasions, when he was halfway up the mountain, he looked ahead up the road and saw a car careening down the hill. His body flooded with adrenaline as he sensed the danger of the oncoming car swaying from one side of the road to the other. His mind raced. Should he stay where he was or move to the other side of the road to avoid a collision? He decided to hold steady and slow down while staying on his side of the road. He was fixated on every move of the oncoming car, and as it got close, he was relieved to see it swing back onto the correct side of the road.

As the other car skimmed past him, a woman stuck her head out the window and screamed, "PIG!" to which he thought, "What! How dare she call me that! Pig? Me, a pig?" Without hesitation, he retaliated at the top of his voice, "SOW!" ... and as he turned the corner, he slammed into a pig!

If you aren't already happy at work, take time to think about your perceptions and expectations. For example, do you, like Ron, automatically believe that people are out to get you? What if they are actually trying to help you?

Consider Dumping some Old Baggage

Some of your perceptions are undoubtedly realistic, while others may be open to interpretation. Which ones can you afford to throw away? Which ones can be replaced with optimistic ideas? Notice your coworker's perceptions too. Look around you: Who's happier? Who's chronically grouchy? Who's celebrating? Who's always sick?

If the place you work in isn't inherently dangerous to your well-being, there is a chance that you can dump some old baggage, change your perceptions, and be happy there. If you're in a place that you recognize as chronically unhealthy and unlikely to change, the best thing you can do for yourself is to look for something better, where you'll be able to provide a Synergy "WOW" Factor! service to your customers there.

Khalil Gibran said, "If you can't love your work, you may as well take up a begging bowl." He wasn't being sarcastic. In Buddhism, there is an idea that the beggar has a natural place in the social order. The beggar allows the rest of us to be generous, which enlarges our spiritual well-being. The beggar is doing us a favor, braving the elements of hunger and the stingy who are not ready to give. The beggar, in this light, according to this perception, is the generous one.

> "Say 'WOW' to the world, and the world will say 'WOW' to you!"

Chapter #8: Examine your Perceptions About Work

Synergy "WOW" Factor!

Chapter Nine: Have a Synergy *"WOW"* Factor! Attitude

"WOW" Factor! people have great attitudes. People love to do business with people they like.

How do you get the "WOW"? You get the "WOW" Factor! by connecting, engaging, exciting, and delighting your customers. Yes, it is all about them. But it is also important to understand that "WOW"ing your customers has a lot to do with your temperament and attitude . . . and how you feel about serving others.

- Do you love helping others?
- Do you enjoy solving problems?
- Do you have the patience to deal with angry, obnoxious people?
- Can you stay calm and professional under pressure?

If you answered "yes" to most of the questions above, you probably love dealing with people and love what you do.

Having the right mental attitude is an outer reflection of your feelings. "Attitude" describes a person's behavior based on how they choose to think and feel about people and life. Regardless of your product or service, "WOW"ing your customer has more to do with your attitude than your customer's attitude.

Understand why having the Right Mental Attitude is so Important

"It's your attitude, more than your aptitude, that will determine your altitude."

-Zig Ziglar

A warm, welcoming smile and an approachable attitude are the shortest distance between two people. These human relations qualities influence perceptions and "WOW" customers.

Chapter #9: Have a Synergy "WOW" Factor! Attitude

All customers expect to be treated respectfully. Moreover, they remember and feel more important and appreciated when treated with more civility and social grace. When we ask customers what is the single most important ingredient that "WOW"ed them about their customer experience, 90% of the time the answer will be, "How I was treated" or "The way they took care of the problem."

In an overflowing world of sameness and relatively "okay" service, to meet someone who stands out for their wonderful attitude is refreshing. More importantly, when we are recognized by that person and treated well, our existence is validated. We feel as if we stand out from the crowd.

Customers will purchase a product that they perceive enhances their value. In a competitive marketplace, "WOW"ing the customer adds value. If two retail outlets sell the same product, more business will go to the outlet that adds value and makes their customers feel valued. Interpersonal communication and human relations still add the greatest value and build referrals and a loyal base of repeat business.

A welcoming attitude is an instant connection bridge, the acceptance doorway that makes our relationships easier and life more abundant.

In this chapter, we'll explore the different aspects that a Synergy "WOW" Factor! attitude includes.

> *"The only disability in life is a bad attitude."*
> -Scott Hamilton

Have an Attitude of Cooperation, Collaboration, and Synergy

Having an attitude of cooperation, collaboration, and Synergy means that you work with your internal and external customers to build trusting relationships that will benefit them, your company, and maybe the community. This, of course, is easier said than done. It begins with the choices you make regarding your personal and work ethic.

Synergy is always ethically based because it considers all players. It focuses on transparency, proactive communication, and cooperation—the behaviors required to create long-term trusting relationships.

The friend of Synergy is right thinking (Synergy **"WOW"** Factor! Principle #4). When you choose what's right, you automatically do what's smart. Be warned, though, self-serving individuals may scorn you or try to fill your head with doubt. There is an unseen enemy of Synergy, service, teamwork, and relationships. This destructive force lurks in every department and is ever-present in our minds. What is it? Self-centered silo thinking!

A person with a silo mentality focuses on self-serving interests and has a defensive "win/lose" attitude. This is wrong thinking and the opposite of an attitude of cooperation and Synergy; it's a limiting, stunted-growth viewpoint. Silos intend to distance and separate. An attitude of cooperation and collaboration are the antidotes to silo thinking. Cooperative, synergistic attitudes and actions break down walls and build bridges between departments and job functions. This, of course, creates a much better experience for customers.

> *"It is amazing what you can accomplish if you do not care who gets the credit."*
> — Harry S. Truman

Love what you Do

> *"If today were the last day of my life, would I want to do what I am about to do today?"*
> —Steve Jobs

Often, the joy of being able to do what you love is more important than your paycheck.

When you love what you do, it shows! It oozes out of every pore in your body. It shines through your enthusiasm and belief in yourself, your products, and your company. Passion and enthusiasm are contagious. They are sensed and seen as an outer reflection of an authentic person of integrity. When you love what you do, customers will see you as someone who genuinely loves and respects the idea of service and enjoys the reciprocal respect and recognition that comes from being thoroughly professional.

You may be fortunate and genuinely love the service business. It may come naturally to you. But not everyone is in a job they love. Many people work jobs to make a living, and if coming to work is not a joyful experience, it makes "WOW"ing the customer more difficult.

If you realize that life is about choices, you understand that you can choose to love what you do—or at least like it a lot, which will have a major impact on how effective you are in "WOW"ing the customer. You are a product of what you think, feel, and do.

Keep in mind that you communicate verbally, visually, and by the "vibe" you generate. The vibe you bring into a room or situation accounts for more than 50% of your communication effectiveness. If you want to "WOW" customers, you need to ramp up your positive energy—and it's easy to have a positive attitude when you love what you do! After all, what you think ("I love my job!") influences how you feel and, in turn, influences your attitude, energy, and actions.

When you love what you do, you naturally put out a lot of positive energy. When you put out positive energy, people are more likely to like being with you. That's why communicating with positive energy can make or break a good customer relationship. When people like you and like being with you, they will feel better about the service and brand. You can be a competitive advantage.

Chapter #9: Have a Synergy "WOW" Factor! Attitude

Be Curious and Inquisitive

We are all born inquisitive and curious—our minds are open. In infancy, you couldn't get enough information! You accepted all information regardless of where it came from. You wanted to know everything. You had a zest for information.

Unfortunately, curiosity and inquisitiveness are natural traits that you can lose as you go through life. Why? Because the curious child, who has constant questions, becomes a nuisance to adults. But when you lose your curiosity, you lose your ability to grow and find solutions and ideas that will enable you to "WOW" your customers.

Be Humble and Grateful

"Gratitude unlocks the door to a fuller life!"

An attitude of gratitude speaks more about the person's character than the act of gratitude itself. Gratitude is a positive, uplifting, and thankful view of life. It says you are happy to be here and grateful for life's smallest blessings.

An attitude of gratitude is a great communication bridge. Gratitude should become a life habit. Maya Angelou, the great author and poet, said that if you look at life through eyes of despair, hate, and anger, that's what your life will be. But if you look at life through eyes of love and gratitude, that's what your life will be.

All too often, though, we cannot feel gratitude because we live in a world where gratitude and thankfulness are seen as weaker, softer elements not to be displayed. We live in sad times when we cannot express how good we have it!

Did you know that the average American family has the best standard of living in the world? Most people have one or even two cars per household, wall-to-wall flooring, chairs, tables, appliances, high levels of entertainment, the latest computer games, the Internet, and access to ample food and highly cost-effective food outlets. We have the fastest service in the world for just about everything.

But the faster we get what we want, the more impatient we become. Many have developed an attitude of instant gratification. They want quick fixes for everything. Quick food, haircuts, books to read, workouts, oil changes, relationships —the list goes on and on. Sadly, expectations based on impatience have led to an attitude of irritation and frustration and, in turn, a lack of gratitude for what they have and a lack of respect for the needs of others and society as a whole.

The solution is not in the speed of life but in the quality of life. Relationships and life have unfortunately been affected by growing self-centeredness—an "I want it now" entitlement attitude.

Chapter #9: Have a Synergy "WOW" Factor! Attitude

Gratitude is about appreciating who we love and who loves us. Gratitude is not being subservient but serving.

"God serves men, but he's not a servant to men."
  -*Eliseo Orefice*, Life Is Beautiful

Gratitude is living in the realm of contribution and service and creating a loving environment. Gratitude and fun are indispensable to living an enriching life. An attitude of gratitude is the essence of joy because it opens your heart and allows you to feel validated and satisfied with life. It keeps you humble and centered and eliminates envy and greed. It helps you recognize the importance of appreciating life despite the moment's circumstances. Gratitude helps you laugh and be merry.

Make it Fun!

"If it's not fun, it's not worth it!"

The Dalai Lama said this about Westerners' focus on their careers:

> *"When I talk to people of various professional backgrounds, particularly from the West, they seem to have a tremendous amount of attachment to their profession . . . people seem to have an enormous personal investment in their profession, they identify with it so much so that they feel as if their profession is so vital for the world's well-being that if it were to degenerate, the whole world would suffer. This seems to me that their level of attachment is inappropriate."*

He's right, of course. We are highly vested in our jobs and what they mean to us. For many of us, it's about who we are. All the more reason to create joy in the workplace!

If you want to create the Synergy "WOW" Factor! in your job, you need to bring your passion and come to work on purpose. Either love your work and feel it's worthwhile, or find something you can become passionate about and make it worthwhile. Obviously, no one will always be delighted with every aspect of their work, but it's vital to have a central core of enjoyment or pleasure so that when things get tough, you still have the emotional security to get you through.

When people come to work because they are having fun and enjoy the people they work with, the organizational culture abounds with positive energy. It becomes a place without fear. A place of play and creativity, growth and development that's oozing with ever-increasing potential. It grows richer, stronger, and more collaborative because of the willingness to work together.

I don't intend to perpetuate the old lie that work is its own reward because it isn't. Passion for your work is its own reward. It rewards you with more than a paycheck. Doing what you love opens the door to having a sense of calmness, including a feeling of rightness with the universe, optimism, and energy beyond just having fun. It's a spiritual experience. You were put on this earth to do something important, to express the finest and most talented parts of yourself.

Your attitude will either make the atmosphere fun and enjoyable for everyone from your co-workers to your customers . . . or it will make the atmosphere awful for one and all. One of the most important factors in having fun and achieving joy in your workplace, is your inner ecology. Just like everything else in life, joy is a choice, and it's intertwined with perception and attitude. How you choose to see things will influence your experience.

As Obi-wan Kenobi said, "Many of the truths we cling to depend greatly on our point of view." Why not choose to make it fun?

Synergy "WOW" Factor!

If you ever watch the Food Network, you'll see people who are in love with their jobs. The chefs talk about the food, compare flavors, colors, and tastes, smell, cook, and have a great time. But the next time you go to a restaurant, look at the chaos, the heat and flames in the kitchen, and the demanding physical aspects of the work. To be a chef, to work all day and half the night on your feet in a hot kitchen with people yelling, dishes clattering, and hungry, cranky customers waiting—well, you'd better love preparing food!

When you love your work and make it fun, it's easy to commit to being great at it, seek out improvements in yourself, and challenge yourself by taking on new tasks or learning new skills. When you are committed in this way, you are modeling passion and commitment to your team. Your commitment to greatness also impacts when you direct your passion toward the most important people in the business: the customers. Exceptional customer service means more than making the customer happy today. It means "WOW"ing them and making that customer a customer for life! Being willing to go the extra mile with your customers will keep them returning.

Researchers who have worked with concepts like joy in the workplace and making work fun have found that people who enjoy their work are healthier, recover more quickly from illness and injury, work more productively, are more creative, and have greater

Chapter #9: Have a Synergy "WOW" Factor! Attitude

self-esteem and emotional balance. People who are happy at work don't need to use their sick leave to take "mental health" days.

Remember, just like everything else in life, happiness is a choice, and doing what you can to make work fun is also a choice. And as research shows, these positive attitudes are not just good for your company and your customers; they're good for you, too . . . it's a triple win!

> *"Making every customer, a customer for life!"*

I have a colleague who once worked for the sales department of the Vermont Teddy Bear Company in Shelburne, Vermont. At Christmas time, this company shifts into high gear, and people rotate positions as necessary.

One day, word came up from the factory floor that there was a great need to get the teddy bears ready for shipping. A few of the salespeople went down to the factory to help out. They played upbeat music for several hours as they brushed, dressed, and boxed teddy bears. They worked as a team and helped each other get each bear presentable and ready to ship. They had a ball! Years later, my colleague still talks about her time at the Vermont Teddy Bear Company as one of her most enjoyable work experiences. The fun of doing something new as a team made work enjoyable, and having fun made the work more easily achievable.

Another great example of making it fun for your teammates and customers is Southwest Airlines, where fun, respect, communication, and excellence are paramount in creating a sense of meaning and joy in the workplace. In my opinion, one of the keys to Southwest's success is that they understand people want to work in an enjoyable environment and that customers like to deal with a company where people enjoy what they are doing and exude enthusiasm.

Laughing and having a fun experience with customers is an important part of Southwest's culture. As such, humor is encouraged at every level of the organization. People are hired for their attitudes and then trained for their skills. Flight attendants are encouraged to make the "in-flight safety lecture" and their other announcements more fun and entertaining. Following are some real examples that have been reported:

"There may be fifty ways to leave your lover, but there are only four ways out of this airplane."

"We do feature a smoking section on this flight. If you must smoke, contact a member of the flight crew, and we will escort you out onto the wing of the airplane."

"Smoking in the lavatories is prohibited. Any person caught smoking in the lavatories will be asked to leave the plane immediately."

Chapter #9: Have a Synergy "WOW" Factor! Attitude

"Should the cabin lose pressure, oxygen masks will drop from the overhead area. Please place the mask over your own mouth and nose before assisting children or adults acting like children."

"As you exit the plane, please make sure to gather all of your belongings. Anything left behind will be distributed evenly among the flight attendants. Please do not leave unwanted children or spouses."

"The last one off the plane must clean it."

"I know, that was quite a bump, and I know what y'all are thinking. I'm here to tell you it wasn't the airline's fault, it wasn't the pilot's fault, it wasn't the flight attendants' fault. It was the asphalt!"

"Welcome aboard Southwest. To operate your seatbelt, insert the metal tab into the buckle and pull tight. It works just like every other seatbelt; if you don't know how to operate one, you probably shouldn't be unsupervised in public. In the event of a sudden loss of cabin pressure, oxygen masks will drop from the ceiling. Stop screaming, grab the mask, and pull it over your face. If you have a small child traveling with you, secure your mask before assisting with theirs. If you are traveling with two small children, decide now which one you love more."

"Weather at our destination is fifty degrees with some broken clouds, but they'll try to have them fixed before we arrive. Thank you, and remember, nobody loves you or your money more than Southwest Airlines."

Synergy "WOW" Factor!

As another travel-related story illustrates, sometimes a little humor can go a long way toward diffusing a difficult situation. In fact, an award should go to this United Airlines gate agent in Denver for being smart and funny and making her point when confronted with a passenger who probably deserved to fly as cargo.

A flight was canceled. A single agent was rebooking a long line of inconvenienced travelers. Suddenly, an angry passenger pushed his way to the desk. He slapped his ticket down on the counter and said, "I have to be on this flight, and it has to be first class."

The agent replied, "I'm sorry, sir. I'll be happy to try to help you, but I've got to help these folks first. Then, I'm sure we'll be able to work something out."

The passenger was unimpressed. He asked loudly so that everyone behind him could hear, "Do you have any idea who I am?"

Without hesitating, the gate agent smiled, grabbed her public address microphone, and said, "May I have your attention, please?" she began, her voice bellowing throughout the terminal. "I have a passenger here at the gate who doesn't know who he is.

If anyone in the airport can help him find out who he is, please come to gate 17."

Everyone laughed, including the angry passenger. Humor won the day! Sometimes, the best way to engage both your internal and external customers is

Chapter #9: Have a Synergy "WOW" Factor! Attitude

to lighten up and let them have fun.

Of course, if you are having fun at work, why not let the customers in on it? Getting customers involved no doubt grows the base of loyalty. Having fun should involve internal and external customers, vendors, and anyone who will benefit from an exciting, fun experience.

> *"To declare up-front that your plans and actions are to "WOW" customers is a powerful declaration of your integrity."*

Synergy "WOW" Factor!

Conclusion

"We take most of the money that we could have spent on paid advertising and instead put it back into the customer experience. Then we let the customers be our marketing."
-Tony Hseih

When your customers experience satisfaction with a product or service, their expectations have been met. To be impressed means their expectations have been exceeded, but being "WOW"ed means they have just experienced exceptional, extraordinary service. When that happens, your customers cannot resist sharing their experiences.

Creating the "WOW" Factor! in business is highly effective when it works from the inside out. Herve Humler, Co-Founder and President of The Ritz-Carlton, said, "I believe in the power of recognition and empowerment. Recognition is the core of our culture and how we achieve outstanding customer service."

Tony Hsieh of Zappos said, "Customer service shouldn't be a department; it should be the entire company."

Synergy "WOW" Factor!

The foundation of a consistent "WOW" Factor! service rests on the entire company synergistically embracing service as a personal and companywide core value. We call this the Spirit of Synergy, the first of the seven Synergy "WOW" Factor! Principles. The Spirit of Synergy is a mindset, a heart connection, and behavior focused on building symbiotic relationships.

The Spirit of Synergy grows quickly in an environment of integrity. It is manifested through the belief that by working together and focusing our talents and abilities on a shared destiny (i.e., goal/vision), we will cause a much greater positive effect on our customers, company, and employees.

$$1+1=3!$$

Peter Drucker said, "Culture eats strategy for breakfast, and for any enlightened leader, the response would be—of course, it does!"

Let me be clear: Service is not a bed of roses. The idea that the customer is always right is a statement that has frustrated many CSRs and salespeople because it is simply not true. The customer is not always right. The customer can be difficult, demanding, and downright rude. But admitting that, doesn't mean we don't want their business or that suddenly we don't care or are not service-oriented. On the contrary, we understand our customers better by not being in denial. We can deal with the reality of knowing that we need to learn to love solving problems and develop interpersonal skills to turn unhappy or difficult customers into loyal customers for life.

Conclusion

Sam Walton of Walmart said, "There is only one boss. The customer! He can fire everybody in the company, from the chairman down, simply by spending his money somewhere else."

- The **goal of Synergy** is to strive for the compounded, mutually beneficial gain achieved from working together in service.

- The **essence of Synergy** is the inspiring shared experience... "WOW," that was great!

- The **foundation of Synergy** is Relationship Trust.

With Synergy and service as foundational core values, nobody cares who gets the credit, and the greatest human motivators are manifested by a sense of belonging, safety, validation, and trust at all levels of the organization.

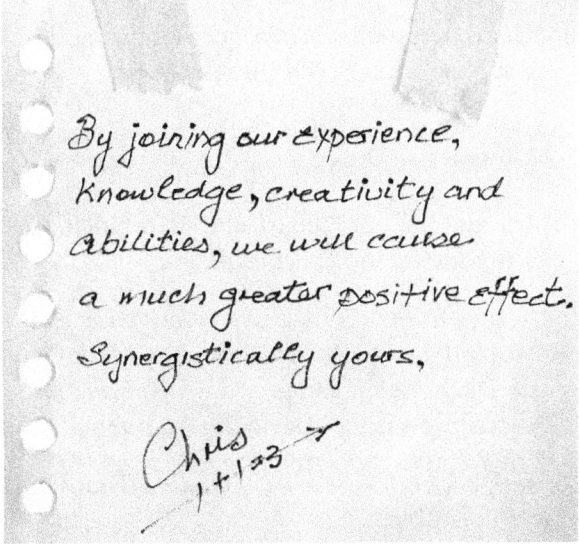

By joining our experience, knowledge, creativity and abilities, we will cause a much greater positive effect. Synergistically yours,

Chris
1+1=3

Bibliography

Albrecht, Carl. *At America's Service.* New York: Warner Books, Inc., 1992.

Alexander, Chris. *Creating Extraordinary Joy.* Alameda, CA: Hunter House, 2001.
———. *Synergizing Your Business.* Lake Forest, CA: 1+1=3 Publishing, 2002.
———. *Joy in the Workplace.* Lake Forest, CA: 1+1=3 Publishing, 2003.
———. *Synergy Strategic Planning.* Lake Forest, CA: 1+1=3 Publishing, 2010.

Allen, James. *As a Man Thinketh.* Mount Vernon, NY: The Peter Pauper Press, n.d.

Barker, Joel Arthur. *Paradigms: The Business of Discovering the Future.* New York: HarperCollins Publishers, Inc., 1992.

Beatty, Jack. *The World According to Peter Drucker.* New York: Free Press, 1998.

Berne, Eric. *Games People Play.* New York: Grove Press, 1964.

Blanchard, Kenneth, and Spencer Johnson. *The One Minute Manager.* New York: Berkley Books, 1982.

Blanchard, Ken, and Sheldon Bowles. *Gung Ho!.* New York: William Morrow and Company, Inc., 1998.

Blanchard, Ken, Jim Ballard, and Fred Finch. *Customer Mania!.* New York: Simon & Schuster, Inc., 2004.

Boelkes, Deb. *The WOW Factor Workplace: How to Create a Best Place to Work Culture.* Narrated by Mark Goulston, Mara Purl, and David Acuff. King's Lynn, UK: Haven Books Audio; Business World Rising LLC, 2020. Audiobook.

Bonstingl, John Jay. *Schools of Quality.* Thousand Oaks, CA: Corwin Press, Inc., 2001.

Branson, Richard. *The Virgin Way: If It's Not Fun, It's Not Worth Doing.* Narrated by Gildart Jackson. New York: Penguin Audio, 2023. Audiobook.

Brown, Stanley A. *Strategic Customer Care: An Evolutionary Approach to Increasing Customer Value and Profitability.* New York: John Wiley & Sons, 2000.

Bruce, Anne, and James S. Pepitone. *Motivating Employees.* Madison, WI: McGraw-Hill, 1999.

Carlson, Jan. *Moments of Truth.* New York: Harper & Row, 1987.

Capodagli, Bill, and Lynn Jackson. *The Disney Way.* New York: McGraw-Hill, 1999.

Charan, Ram. *Know-How.* New York: Random House, Inc., 2007.
———. *What the Customer Wants You to Know: How Everybody Needs to Think Differently about Sales.* Narrated by Dick Hill. Old Saybrook, CT: Tantor Audio, 2008. Audiobook.

Clear, James. *Atomic Habits: An Easy & Proven Way to Build Good Habits & Break Bad Ones.* New York: Penguin Audio, 2018. Audiobook.

Cockerell, Dan. *How's the Culture in Your Kingdom?: Lessons from a Disney Leadership Journey.* Narrated by Jody Maberry. New York: Morgan James Publishing, 2020. Audiobook.

Collins, James C., and Jerry I. Porras. *Built to Last.* New York: HarperCollins Publishers Inc., 1994.

Collins, Jim. *Good to Great.* New York: HarperCollins Publishers Inc., 2001.

Covey, Stephen R. *The 7 Habits of Highly Effective People.* New York: Simon & Schuster, Inc., 1990.
———. *Principle-Centered Leadership.* New York: Simon & Schuster, Inc., 1992.

Covey, Stephen M. R. *The Speed of Trust: The One Thing that Changes Everything.* New York: Simon & Schuster Audio, 2008. Audiobook.

Coyle, Daniel. *The Culture Code: The Secrets of Highly Successful Groups.* Narrated by Will Damron. New York: Random House Audio, 2018. Audiobook.

Delorenzo, Richard A., Wendy J. Battino, Rick M. Schreiber, and Carrio. *Delivering on the Promise.* Bloomington, IN: Solution Tree, 2009.

Denove, Chris, and James D. Power IV. *Satisfaction.* New York: Penguin Group, 2006.

DeVos, Rich. *Compassionate Capitalism.* New York: Penguin Group, 1994.

Drucker, Peter F. *The New Realities.* New York: Harper & Row, 1989.
———. *The Effective Executive.* New York: Harper & Row, 1996.
———. *Management Challenges for the Twenty First Century.* New York: HarperCollins Publishers Inc., 1999.

Duhigg, Charles. T*he Power of Habit: Why We Do What We Do in Life and Business.* New York: Random House, Inc., 2012. Audiobook.

Freiberg, Kevin, and Jackie Freiberg. *Nuts! Southwest Airlines' Crazy Recipe for Business and Personal Success.* Austin, TX: Bard Press, 1996.

Fuller, R. Buckminster. *Synergetics: Explorations in the Geometry of Thinking.* New York: Macmillan Publishers, 1975.

Gitomer, Jeffrey. *Customer Satisfaction is Worthless.* Austin, TX: Bard Press, 1998.

Gittell, Jody Hoffer. *The Southwest Airlines Way.* Narrated by Anna Fields. New York: McGraw Hill-Ascent Audio, 2022. Audiobook.

Godin, Seth. *This Is Marketing: You Can't Be Seen Until You Learn to See.* New York: Penguin Audio, 2018. Audiobook.

Goldstein, Sheldon D. *Superior Customer Satisfaction and Loyalty.* Milwaukee, WI: ASQ Quality Press, 2004.

Goleman, Daniel. *Emotional Intelligence.* New York: Bantam Books, 1995.

Goleman, Daniel, Richard Boyatzis, and Annie McKee. *Primal Leadership: Learning to Lead with Emotional Intelligence.* Boston, MA: Harvard Business School, 2002.

Grant, Adam M. Give and Take: *A Revolutionary Approach to Success. Narrated by Brian Keith Lewis.* New York: Penguin Audio, 2013. Audiobook.

Greene, Robert. *The Laws of Human Nature.* Narrated by Paul Michael. New York: Penguin Audio, 2018. Audiobook.

Greenleaf, Robert K. *On Becoming a Servant Leader.* Edited by Don M. Frick and Larry C. Spears. San Francisco, CA: Jossey-Bass Publishers, 1996.

Greiner, Donna, and Theodore B. Kinni. *1,001 Ways to Keep Customers Coming Back.* New York: Crown Business, 1999.

Guidara, Will. *Unreasonable Hospitality: The Remarkable Power of Giving People More than They Expect.* New York: Penguin Audio, 2022. Audiobook.

Hardy, Darren. *The Compound Effect: Multiply Your Success One Simple Step at a Time.* New York: Folio Literary Management, 2019. Audiobook.

Henson, Jim. *It's Not Easy Being Green.* New York, NY: Hyperion, 2005.

Henricks, Mark. *Grow Your Business.* Irvine, CA: Entrepreneur Press, 2001.

Hill, Napoleon. *Think and Grow Rich.* North Hollywood, CA: Wilshire Book Company, 1966.

———. *Law of Success.* Chicago, IL: Success Unlimited, Inc., 1979.

Hilton, Conrad. *Be My Guest.* New York, NY: Fireside, 1994.

Hsieh, Tony. *Delivering Happiness: A Path to Profits, Passion, and Purpose.* New York: Hachette Audio, 2010. Audiobook.

Hyken, Shep. *Amaze Every Customer Every Time: 52 Tools for Delivering the Most Amazing Customer Service on the Planet.* Narrated by Joe Bronzi. Newark: Audible Studios, 2014. Audiobook.

Lencioni, Patrick. *The Five Dysfunctions of a Team.* San Francisco, CA: Jossey-Bass Publishers, 2002.

Loehr, Jim, and Tony Schwartz. *The Power of Full Engagement.* New York: Free Press, 2003.

Lowenstein, Michael W. *The Customer Advocate and the Customer Saboteur.* Seattle: Quality Press, 2011.

Maxwell, John C. *25 Ways to Win with People: How to Make Others Feel like a Million Bucks.* Narrated by Les Parrott and Henry O. Arnold. New York: HarperCollins Leadership, 2020. Audiobook.

McBride, Linda. *The Mass Market Woman.* Eagle River, AK: Crowded Hour Press, 1999.

Miller, Donald. *Building a Story Brand: Clarify Your Message So Customers Will Listen.* New York: HarperCollins Leadership, 2017. Audiobook.

Moore, Thomas. *Original Self.* New York: HarperCollins Publishers Inc., 1981.

Nerburn, Kent, and Louise Mengelkoch. *Native American Wisdom.* San Rafael, CA: New World Library, 1991.

Performance Research Associates. *Delivering Knock Your Socks Off Service*. Illustrated by John Bush. New York: AMACOM, 2011.

Pearsall, Paul. *The Pleasure Prescription*. Alameda, CA: Hunter House, 1998.

Peck, M. Scott. *The Road Less Traveled*. New York: Simon & Schuster, Inc., 1978.

Peters, Tom. *The Pursuit of Wow: Every Person's Guide to Topsy-Turvy Times*. Narrated by the author. New York: Random House Audio, 2006. Audiobook.

Robbins, Anthony. *Awaken the Giant Within*. New York: Summit Books, 1991.

Rowley, Laura. *On Target: How the World's Hottest Retailer Hit a Bull's-Eye*. New York: John Wiley & Sons, 2009.

Schein, Edgar H. *Organizational Culture and Leadership*. San Francisco, CA: Jossey-Bass, 2004.

Schultz, Howard, Joanne Gordon, and Stephen Bowlby. *Onward: How Starbucks Fought for Its Life Without Losing Its Soul*. Narrated by Stephen Bowlby. Charlotte Hall, MD: HighBridge, a division of Recorded Books, 2011. Audiobook.

Senge, Peter M. *The Fifth Discipline*. New York: Doubleday, 1994.

Sewell, Carl, and Paul B. Brown. *Customers for Life: How to Turn That One-Time Buyer into a Lifetime Customer*. New York: Crown Currency, 2002.

Shaw, Robert Bruce. *Trust in the Balance: Building Successful Organizations on Results, Integrity, and Concern*. San Francisco, CA: Jossey-Bass, 1997.

Sinek, Simon. *The Infinite Game*. New York: Penguin Audio, 2018. Audiobook.
———. *Start with Why: How Great Leaders Inspire Everyone to Take Action*. New York: Penguin Audio, 2017. Audiobook.

Spector, Robert, and Patrick D. McCarthy. *The Nordstrom Way: The Inside Story of America's #1 Customer Service Company.* New York: John Wiley & Sons, Inc., 1995.

Stemberg, Thomas G. *Staples for Success.* Santa Monica, CA: Knowledge Exchange, 1996.

Thomas, R. David. *Dave's Way.* New York: Berkley Books, 1992.

Thompson, Harvey. *The Customer-Centered Enterprise.* New York, NY: McGraw-Hill, 2000.

Tracy, Brian. *The 100 Absolutely Unbreakable Laws of Business Success.* San Francisco, CA: Berrett-Koehler Publishers, Inc., 2000.

Vaynerchuk, Gary. *Crushing It!: How Great Entrepreneurs Build Their Business and Influence—and How You Can, Too.* Narrated by Rich Roll and Amy Schmittauer. New York: HarperAudio, 2018. Audiobook.

Whiteley, Richard C. T*he Customer-Driven Company*. Reading, MA: Addison-Wesley Publishing Company, 1992.

Willink, Jocko, and Leif Babin. *Extreme Ownership: How U.S. Navy SEALs Lead and Win.* Narrated by the authors. New York: Macmillan Audio, 2015. Audiobook.

About the Author

Chris Alexander

M.A. (Org. Psych.)

Professional Speaker, Award-Winning Business-Building Strategist and Author

If you want your audience using words like "World-Class," "Outstanding," "Impressive," and "Inspiring," then engage Chris Alexander—a dynamic conference speaker, transformational educator, and Emmy Award-winning thought leader.

With over 30 years of real-world business experience, Chris blends his renowned business success into powerful messages, engaging humor, and actionable strategies that stick. He's a trusted advisor and speaker for global brands like Mercedes-Benz, Barratt American, Johnson & Johnson, and Interior Specialists, Inc.

Chris is a leading authority on:
- Building high-performance cultures
- World-class customer service
- Leadership and synergy-driven teamwork

Through custom retreats, interactive workshops, and long-term partnerships, he helps organizations design energized, aligned cultures that create lasting impacts.

Signature Topics Include:

- Synergy Leadership
- Synergy "WOW" Factor!
- Synergy Team Power
- Synergy Strategic Planning
- Synergy Communication Styles

Chris says *"Synergy is that magic moment when a team moves as one—toward a shared destiny. Communication flows. Energy multiplies. Everyone feels connected, inspired, and unstoppable."*

From Africa to America: A Synergy Story

Chris Alexander was born in Rhodesia—now Zimbabwe—in a village where resources were scarce, but dreams ran deep. Even as a young boy, he sensed that there was more to life than survival; there was significance. He imagined a future where voices mattered, and ideas moved mountains. So, he followed that spark—first across cultures, then across continents.

Arriving in the United States, Chris brought with him more than heritage. He carried a mission: to speak boldly about synergy, alignment, and the extraordinary power of people united in purpose. From small beginnings to Emmy-winning broadcasts and Fortune

500 boardrooms, his journey is proof that geography doesn't limit greatness—it shapes it.

Today, that global perspective infuses every keynote, coaching session, and workshop. Chris doesn't just speak about transformation—he embodies it.

He is the author of Catch the Wind with Your Wings, Creating Extraordinary Joy, Joy in the Workplace, and the acclaimed Synergy series of Books; Synergy Team Power, Synergy "WOW" Factor!, Synergy Leadership, Synergy Strategic Planning and the Synergizing your Business handbook.

His PBS specials Creating Extraordinary Joy and Joy in the Workplace have reached over 4.5 million viewers per broadcast. As part of a team of the Emmy-winning series Dollar$ and Sense: Personal Finance for the 21st Century, he made business education both accessible and unforgettable.

With rich global experience, powerful storytelling, and a message that moves people to act, Chris Alexander doesn't just speak—he ignites transformation. Audiences don't just remember him... they request him by name.

Book Chris Alexander Today!
Let the Synergy begin!

SynergyTeamPower.com
CAlexander@SynergyTeamPower.com

www.ingramcontent.com/pod-product-compliance
Lightning Source LLC
Chambersburg PA
CBHW060116170426
43198CB00010B/909